T0157701

Faith, Hope, Courage, and New Beginnings

100 Devotional Writings

STEPHANIE MURPHY

WESTBOW
PRESS®
A DIVISION OF THOMAS NELSON
& ZONDERVAN

WestBow Press books may be ordered through booksellers or by contacting:

WestBow Press
A Division of Thomas Nelson & Zondervan
1663 Liberty Drive
Bloomington, IN 47403
www.westbowpress.com
1 (866) 928-1240

ISBN: 978-1-5127-9843-2 (sc)
ISBN: 978-1-5127-9844-9 (hc)
ISBN: 978-1-5127-9842-5 (e)

Library of Congress Control Number: 2017912522

Print information available on the last page.

WestBow Press rev. date: 08/25/2017

To _____

From _____

Dedication

*I dedicate this book to my husband, Eric,
and to my son, my daughter,
and my grandchildren.*

Contents

Part 1

Part 2

Part 3

Part 4

Preface

Over the years, God has inspired me to write from my heart. I have to admit that, at times, I feel quite vulnerable doing this, but I have continued to write in spite of the vulnerability, leaving the outcome in God's hands.

My purpose for writing this book was to share how good and faithful God is in the midst of all that makes up our lives on this earth. Life can be difficult. Yet God promises us that He is with us and cares about our hurts. We all experience loss, in one form or another, during the course of our lives. Yet this very loss leads us to faith, hope, courage, and new beginnings.

In this book, I share my reflections on love, loss, marriage, spiritual growth, and worship. I share insights from my personal and professional experience and from the wisdom of God's Word. More specifically, I touch on the loss of a spouse through death, remarriage later in life, and how we are led to a closer walk with God in the midst of our brokenness.

It is my hope that my writings will encourage you and help shed light on situations that many of us have in common. I want to share how good and faithful God is to His children. It is my prayer that this book will be a blessing to you.

Acknowledgments

I want to thank my husband, Eric, my children, and my grandchildren. I am grateful for their love and encouragement and the life experiences we've shared together. I am especially thankful for Eric's daily proofreading and his encouragement to "keep on writing!"

I am grateful for my friend Gene Cogdill's encouragement to write my first blog and for my friends, who walked closely beside me during my time of grief right up to my marriage and the time of new beginnings. I appreciate their continued support as I join my husband in his life's work as a missionary to young people in Europe and Costa Rica.

I am especially thankful for my lifelong friend, Leslie Camp, who first invited me to church when I was a child. This led me to accept Christ as my Savior. Our friendship has deepened over the course of fifty years.

A special thanks to my dear friends, Ed and Cathi Blair, who watched over me as I walked through those early weeks and months of widowhood. I am forever grateful to all of my Christian friends, who became an extension of God's love to me. You know who you are.

God impressed on my heart, many years ago, that He

wanted to bless me and make me a blessing to others. I believe this is true for all of us, in our own special ways. My prayer is that God will bless each of you and make you a blessing to those around you.

Tribute

As I'm writing about new beginnings, I want to take the time to honor the memories of my late husband, Jerry, and Eric's late wife, Lynne. Jerry moved to heaven on March 12, 2014. He was loved by everyone who knew him and always put a smile on people's faces. Lynne moved to heaven on December 5, 2013, after a long battle with multiple sclerosis. She served alongside Eric as a missionary in Hungary for many years and was also a gifted musician.

Recently, a dear friend shared with me that, just a few days before Jerry moved to heaven, he called him into his hospital room. Jerry told him how sad and worried he was about leaving me. He asked him to promise that he and his wife would keep an eye on me and help me.

Then Jerry went on to say that his desire for me was that I always remember his love for me, *but* that I would not mourn for him too long and would find someone who would love me and make me happy. So these friends have told me, "We see Eric as an answer to prayer—ours *and* Jerry's." When I visited Eric's family church in West Virginia, the Easter before Eric and I were married, a woman came up to me, greeted me, and said, "You're an answer to Lynne's prayer."

PART 1

Hope Renewed

And we know that all things work together for good to them that love God, to them who are the called according to *his* purpose.

—Romans 8:28 (KJV)

In my fifties, I felt I had God's blessing on my life. I believed that God was blessing me abundantly at this stage because I had already gone through difficult times earlier. I truly believed God was giving me hope and a future.

I had a husband who adored me, a ministry and career as a Christian counselor, two grown children, and three beautiful grandchildren. I had a wonderful church and many loyal friends. I wanted for nothing and felt secure. My life felt stable and purposeful. I had a close relationship with the Lord and felt content in my soul.

Then suddenly, within a three-month period, everything changed. My husband became ill and was hospitalized. Three months later, I was preparing for his funeral.

I was shocked and disbelieved this could happen. I thought God must hate me to take my husband from me, along with my secure, peaceful life. I went through a year of intense grief. But with God's help, I did what I needed to do to emerge from the grief whole.

It was an interesting journey filled with many lessons and deep spiritual growth. I learned to trust God's providence and to trust Him again with my future. I learned to walk closely with Him and to allow Him to fill me with His peace.

After my year of grief, I knew in my heart that I was ready to love again. I was ready for God to repurpose my life. As I opened my heart to receive all that God had for me, my circumstances began to change. I met a kindhearted man who is now my husband. Along with this wonderful man, God gave me the opportunity to be a part of mission work. The man God chose for me is a missionary, and I have been walking alongside him in his work.

I now have renewed hope in God's promise to give us hope and a future. I may never fully understand why I experienced the things I went through in life. I only know that God meant them for my good. I now look forward to the new life He has for me.

If your hope has been shaken by circumstances beyond your control, I pray that you find renewed hope in His promise that all things work together for our good. May you find renewed hope for the future He has for you!

2

Blessed New Year

"For I know the plans I have for you," declares the Lord, "plans to prosper you and not to harm you, plans to give you hope and a future."

—Jeremiah 29:11 (NIV)

Jeremiah 29:11 describes what most of us hope for. Many of us take time to think through and write out *our* plans and goals for each new year, but how about the plans *God* has for us? We don't always think of it this way, do we? Instead, we rack our brains for ways to improve ourselves and our lives. There's nothing wrong with that as long as we balance it with our trust in God's plans for us. He has plans to bless us and not to harm us.

I've never really had the desire to be rich—only blessed. I love it when I feel blessed and know in my heart that it isn't just luck or even hard work, but it is from the hand of God. In recent years, I have learned to see God's blessings even in difficult circumstances. I can now accept that they are for my good.

Not everyone faces a new year with hope. Many deal with illnesses, relationship problems, or financial insecurity. Yet God says that He has plans to give us hope. Maybe we can be an extension of God's love to others—to give them hope, to show them love, or to lighten their load. God says that along with hope, He plans to give us a future.

When we're young, it seems easy to look forward to a bright future since so many opportunities and adventures are still ahead of us. But how about those of us who are farther along in life? We've raised our families, finished our formal education, and worked in our careers. What then?

Again, God says He has plans to give us a future. Although I've basically retired from my professional counseling career, I'm not finished yet. I believe God isn't finished with me yet. I see adventures and experiences ahead of me. I still have work to do, people to love and care for, and certainly, room to grow.

I am thankful to God for the plans He has for me—plans to bless me and not to harm me. I pray that you will begin each new year with the hope of a blessed future!

First Holiday Alone

He heals the brokenhearted and binds up their wounds.

—Psalm 147:3 (NASB)

Today I am thinking of those who are facing their first holiday alone. I am saying a prayer for you and asking God to comfort your heart during this time. Many of you will have strong arms of love around you from family and friends. Others will not.

Some of you will have a large and supportive extended family. Others, who have no one close by, may truly feel that when they are alone, they are *really* alone. Regardless of your circumstances, it is a difficult time. You may be overwhelmed with tears as memories flood your mind and heart. Don't be afraid of tears. They can be a healing balm.

Your first holiday alone can feel awkward, as others seem to go on with their normal lives—everyone but you! I found people to be sensitive and kind. Many offered to accompany me to social events, but sometimes, I chose to stay at home. Although you shouldn't become a hermit, it's okay to bow out of some social activities that may make you feel uncomfortable or sad. Be gentle with yourself.

It may feel as though there's a big hole in your heart without your loved one by your side. Nothing on this earth seems to fill the void. I found my comfort in the spiritual rather than in my physical, earthly surroundings. That isn't to say, the calls and words of encouragement from family and friends weren't helpful. Each was tremendously appreciated and brought warmth into my life during that dark time.

But my deep comfort and help came from pressing into God. I literally felt the prayers of others holding me up when my heart was weighed down with grief. As I drew closer to God, read His Word, and called on the name of Jesus, I received strength. That strength took the form of faith, hope, and courage.

Yes, I survived my first holidays as a widow. Was it easy? Not at all! Did I grow from it? Absolutely! Looking back, I can definitely say, "All things work together for good to those who love God," as the Bible tells us. God has been faithful, and my hope has been restored.

I hope you, also, will press into God and allow Him to walk beside you on your grief journey. I pray that your hope will be renewed for all the days ahead of you.

Beauty for Ashes

To appoint unto them that mourn in Zion, to give unto them beauty for ashes, the oil of joy for mourning, the garment of praise for the spirit of heaviness; that they might be called trees of righteousness, the planting of the Lord, that He might be glorified.

—Isaiah 61:3 (KJV)

If the Christmas season finds you in mourning, I want to encourage you. God wants to give you beauty for ashes, joy in place of mourning, and the garment of praise instead of the spirit of heaviness. He wants to make a trade with you.

There is a time for grieving and mourning the loss of a loved one. There is also a time to trade your heavy heart for a heart of praise and to allow God to give you beauty for ashes and to turn your mourning into joy.

This may seem impossible to you if you are overwhelmed with feelings of sadness and loss. I am well aware of the tendency for those feelings to become intensified during the holidays. That's all the more reason to press into God and to find hope and encouragement in His Word.

If you have experienced great loss in your life, be assured that God has not forgotten about you. He sees every tear and hears the cry of your heart. Remember that you are never alone. He is right where you are at this moment.

Each December marks the anniversary of the death of my husband's first wife, Lynne. Every March signifies another year since my late husband, Jerry, moved to heaven. Eric and I both know the sting of loss as we remember those difficult days, yet we are both at peace and are wonderfully happy in our marriage and our life together.

During each holiday season, our loved ones come to our minds and are forever in our hearts. But it is different now. We know their suffering is over and they are the happiest they have ever been. They are in the presence of Jesus. We have traded our mourning for joy, and God has truly given us beauty for ashes. For that, I am thankful.

Finding Rest

Come to me, all you who are weary and burdened, and I
will give you rest.

—Matthew 11:28 (NIV)

Yes, He has provided us with all that we need to rest from
the burdens of life. As we lay our problems and our
failures at His feet, we find peace. Resolutions and goals bring
some of us face-to-face with what we perceive as failure—
blown diets, lack of exercise, or neglecting our prayer times.

Some of our goals have gone by the wayside. Then comes
the guilt! We beat ourselves up for not being stronger, vowing
to try harder tomorrow. So what do we do? Instead of *trying
harder*, we need to press into Jesus more. He died for our
failures and our brokenness. He's the only one who can give
us the power we need to change from the inside out.

Most of us don't really follow through with our new
resolutions. Why? Because we depend on willpower, and
willpower has its limits.

God has given us the power of the Holy Spirit to help us become more and more like Jesus as we walk through life on this earth. The Bible teaches us to be filled with the Spirit and to walk in the Spirit and not in the flesh. So don't just *try harder* but press into God more.

I am thankful Christ invites us to come to Him, not only for salvation but also for strength, rest, and peace. May God strengthen you as you draw closer to Him, and may you find peace as you rest in Him.

A Surrendered Life

Then Jesus said to his disciples, "Whoever wants to be my disciple must deny themselves and take up their cross and follow me. For whoever wants to save their life will lose it, but whoever loses their life for me will find it."

—Matthew 16:24–25 (NIV)

This pretty much describes a surrendered life, doesn't it? One night, as we sang the old hymn "I Surrender All" in church, I couldn't help but glance at the wooden cross hanging up front and reflect on what Jesus had surrendered for me—everything!

I thought about my own life and how I had recently married a missionary and had dedicated myself to be a missionary with him. Then I thought about what I had surrendered and realized that it paled in comparison to what Jesus had laid down on Calvary's cross.

As followers of Christ, we may find that our life choices don't always elicit the full support of our family and friends.

We may try to explain ourselves, defend ourselves, and structure our *new normal* in the most positive way we can. However, when our own efforts seem to fail, we have to surrender those relationships to God and trust Him with the outcome.

God calls all of us as believers to live a life surrendered to Him and to His will. It is in the beauty of this surrender that He can fully bless our lives and make us a blessing to others. It is my desire to continue to trust Him, knowing that His ways are greater than my ways, and His thoughts are higher than my thoughts.

I am thankful that God has richly blessed me and has repurposed my life. I am humbled by the opportunity to join my husband in his life's work. What a rich experience it has already been. I pray for God's blessing on each of you as you endeavor to live a surrendered life.

Peace in His Presence

I have told you these things, so that in me you may have peace. In the world you will have trouble. But take heart! I have overcome the world.

—John 16:33 (NIV)

Some of us experience this "trouble" in the form of family difficulties or marital conflicts. Others struggle with financial problems or health issues. But Jesus says that in Him we can have peace!

For many years, I counseled people who were experiencing anxiety and depression. They felt powerless and overwhelmed by their circumstances. Their main symptom seemed to be a lack of peace. Basically, a sense of fear and unrest permeated their emotional outlook, and many had simply given up.

Bouts of anxiety or depression can be either acute or chronic. With acute anxiety or depression, feelings are usually brought on by a particular event or experience. Symptoms dissipate rather quickly when issues are resolved.

Chronic anxiety or depression becomes the norm for some people. Symptoms may not be as intense as in acute cases, but a person's sense of well-being is disrupted over longer periods. This kind of depression or anxiety is often associated with a person's thought patterns (in other words, the lens through which they view life).

As Christians, we have God's Word as a basis for our outlook on life. We are offered peace in His presence. Sometimes we take it for granted and don't avail ourselves of this provision. We forget that, as followers of Christ, God has equipped us with all we need to live victoriously in this world.

These past few years have been a time of spiritual growth for me—a time of learning to find peace in His presence instead of looking for it in perfect circumstances. I am very thankful for all of God's blessings, but I've learned that it is important to find peace in His presence, even when all seems well and His blessings are flowing into my life. You see, it is His *presence* and not the blessing itself that brings peace. It is my prayer that each of you will find peace in His presence regardless of your circumstances.

Change

Do not conform to the pattern of this world, but be transformed by the renewing of your mind. Then you will be able to test and approve what God's will is—his good, pleasing and perfect will.

—Romans 12:2 (NIV)

Transformation! *Change*! As Christians, we are constantly being transformed into Christ's likeness. These changes may result from prayer and Bible study, or they may come from life experiences.

Now that I'm in the second half of my life, these experiences have taken on new meaning for me. My grown children sometimes say that I've changed. My answer is always, "Yes, life experiences change us—hopefully for the better" (You can't go through the illness and death of a spouse without being changed or the diagnosis of a grandchild with autism without being broken).

Without a doubt, the inevitable hurts we experience in

life produce change, however, so do the many blessings we receive. How we bend in the midst of life's storms creates either a resilient person or a resentful one. We all have been broken by suffering or loss, but the effect we allow that brokenness to have on us determines the outcome.

I've found that we can also be changed by the blessings we receive in life. We either become more grateful or merely take those blessings for granted, thinking we need more before we can be happy. I have chosen to be grateful for God's blessings. I appreciate them even more after having experienced loss.

My faith has deepened. My hope has been renewed. I have found courage I never knew I had. God has restored what was lost and has given me a new beginning, even at this stage in my life. As I write from a deeper place in my heart, I now have the courage to be a bit more vulnerable. So yes, I suppose I have changed.

My prayer is that each of you will be transformed more and more into the image of Christ as you follow Him. May you press into Him and find peace, courage, and hope in the midst of life's storms.

Healing Love

And he arose, and rebuked the wind, and said unto the sea, Peace, be still. And the wind ceased, and there was great calm.

—Mark 4:39 (KJV)

I've written a lot about God's healing love over the past few years. It seems to be what God keeps bringing me back to. I started writing about healing love after my grandson was diagnosed with autism several years ago. This wasn't my first response, but it was the place God brought me to. I went from a position of disbelief, grief, and bargaining with God to a place of acceptance and peace.

I see my grandson as a beautiful gift and feel privileged that God entrusted me to be his grandmother. My prayer for him is that he will feel happy, loved, and accepted and that he will reach his full God-given potential. It is my desire to be an extension of God's love to him.

I wrote again about God's healing love, after my late

husband, Jerry, moved to heaven. It took God's healing love to bring me through the storm of grief I was going through.

Mark 4:35–41 tells the story of Jesus calming the stormy sea when His disciples came to Him for help. They didn't come in perfect faith. In fact, they came in *fear*. Jesus met them where they were and understood their need for peace and calm. He said to the stormy sea, "Peace, be still."

As I walked, day by day, through my grief, God sent His healing love to me in many different ways. I felt His love through the encouraging texts, notes, and cards, which were sent by friends and family during those weeks and months, and through the telephone calls of friends from hundreds of miles away, which came at just the right time.

God also gave me a hearty dose of His healing love in the *GriefShare* group I was a part of for thirteen weeks. I remember desperately needing to be around someone who was going through what I was experiencing. My couple friends were great and supportive, but the desire to share with others who knew exactly what I was going through, burned inside me.

A supportive *Hospice* counselor was also a manifestation of God's healing love during that time. She listened and told me that what I was feeling was "normal" for my circumstance and assured me that I wasn't losing my mind.

My journey of grief was a storm, but God came through for me and met me where I was. I realized, early on, that I couldn't find peace in my own strength. I had to start walking in the present with my big God, with my God who can do anything. Now I can look back and clearly see all the amazing gifts of love God showered upon me. I will always be grateful for His healing love.

God's healing love has continued to manifest itself in my life through restoration and new beginnings. My marriage to Eric is an extension of God's love for me. God has given me the opportunity to love again and to have new purpose in my life. God has taught me that His healing love is all around me and I can be an extension of His love to others.

I have a feeling that God will bring me back, again and again, to His healing love throughout the rest of my days on this earth. You see, this love flows freely to us throughout the circumstances of our lives as we press into God rather than become angry or bitter toward Him. He sees our hurts, but He is with us.

If you are in your own stormy sea of grief, hurt, or loss, it is my hope and prayer that you will look to God and allow Him to shower you with His precious healing love. Don't wait until your faith is perfect. He will meet you where you are, calm your storm, and give you His peace!

10

Walking Each Other Home

In my Father's house are many mansions: if *it were* not *so*, I would have told you. I go to prepare a place for you.

—John 14:2 (KJV)

Jesus is talking about home—our *eternal* home! Some of us have experienced the illness and death of a loved one. We were by their side during the dark days. We cared for and supported them until they reached their destination. We walked them home.

I hadn't thought of it this way—that we're all just *walking each other home*. The words resonated with me as I reflected on the journey I had walked with Jerry during the last few months of his life. As I thought about Eric's journey with Lynne through her final days on this earth, I realized that we walked them home.

Our presence made their journey a little less frightening—helped them feel a little less alone. Only God could truly comfort their souls, but we were an extension of His love to them. We walked them home.

Most of us have experienced walking somewhere unfamiliar in the dark. Even though we know we will eventually arrive at a safe place, we welcome the company of a trusted friend.

As a child, when kids still played outside after dark, we sometimes took turns walking each other home. It's an act of love—sacrificial love, at times—to walk someone home. You set aside your own needs, not out of obligation but from a deeper place—a place of knowing, *This is what they need right now.* You know in your heart that what you are doing has deep purpose, no matter how tedious or unglamorous it may seem.

I think we have to realize that we are walking each other home throughout all our lives and not just at the end of our days on this earth. So let's be a little kinder to each other along the way—a little less critical, a little more loving.

Life is messy at times. People can be messy. But love transcends the messiness as we walk each other home!

11

Back to the Shore

And he arose, and came to his father. But when he was
a great way off, his father saw him, and had compassion,
and ran, and fell on his neck, and kissed him.

—Luke 15:20 (KJV)

I've met some people who have accepted Christ at an earlier
time in their lives but, for one reason or another, have lost
their way. My husband and I have a heart for these people. We
don't judge them, but instead, we reach out to them in love.
We see their potential and genuinely want to encourage them.

I saw this same dynamic over and over during the three
decades I practiced as a professional Christian counselor and
marriage therapist. Good people were floundering in their
lives. Even though they knew that they had taken the wrong
path, they couldn't seem to find their way back. I gave the
analogy that they had gradually waded out too far into the
water. By the time they looked back, they could no longer
see the shore. There was no light.

Many of us have had times in our lives when we have experienced this. It's frightening for those who have walked in the light to wake up, longing for the safety and security of the shore. That shore can seem so very far away, but it is closer than you think. It is one sincere prayer away!

If you are the person I have just described, I would encourage you to begin your journey back to the shore. "But how?" you ask. My answer is for you to start right where you are. Begin to talk to God again. Your heavenly Father will meet you there. You don't have to desperately flail about in an effort to swim back to the shore in your own strength.

God wants a relationship with you. Start by praying and opening yourself up to renewing your relationship with Him. If you need forgiveness, ask for it. Don't worry about what other people think. Genuine Christians will accept you just as our Father accepts you—with open arms! Focus your eyes on Him as you go back to the shore of His love and grace.

12

Your Maker Is Your Husband

And remember no more the reproach of your widowhood.
For your Maker is your husband—the Lord Almighty is
his name—the Holy One of Israel is your Redeemer; he
is called the God of all the earth.

—Isaiah 54:4–5 (NIV)

One day, I bumped into a friend I hadn't seen for a while.
She had become a widow that past year. I immediately
sensed that her spirit was down—she was broken. I just
wanted to hug her and give her encouragement.

I whispered a prayer for her, asking God to help her find
peace, hope, and even joy again. I asked God to help her see
that our peace comes from His presence and not from our
circumstances. I prayed that He would help her to press into
Him rather than fear the future.

My friend needed strength. She was at the end of her own
supply. I knew those feelings well. Losing her husband of

many years had suddenly left her without the companionship and emotional support on which she had come to rely.

Early on in my own grief process, I had joined a single women's Bible study. Some had never been married while others had been widowed or divorced. I will never forget the leader's confident statement the first time I visited the group. "God is my husband," she said. She meant it, and she lived it! She could smile, laugh, and reach out to others. She was at peace despite her difficult circumstances. Her attitude made an impact on me as I pondered her statement.

During my months of grief, I leaned into God, allowing Him to be my husband. I found Him to be faithful in His love and care for me during my time of need. I am grateful that He helped me understand that He was walking beside me and going before me.

I am thankful for His many blessings, including the sweet, godly husband He sent into my life. He has given me not only peace but also hope for my future. He has restored my joy!

If you are in the midst of your own storm of grief and widowhood, I pray that you allow your Maker to be your husband. May you find new joy as you look forward to all the days He has ahead for you.

13

Let Go

Precious in the sight of the Lord *is* the death of His saints.

—Psalm 116:15 (KJV)

While coming to terms with the loss of my spouse through death, I wrote the following passage to reframe my experience of grief into the beautiful transformation that takes place for believers.

> Who am I that my temporal happiness or comfort should get in the way of the glorious transformation that has taken place for Jerry? He has reached his ultimate destiny, transformed to perfection by Christ and now living in his designated area of our Father's house with countless others, angels, and Jesus. Like the caterpillar who leaves the shell behind to burst forth and fly away as a beautiful butterfly, he's not the same person I shared my life with.
>
> The same spirit and personality are now perfected—all the good without the human failings. How beautiful

he must be. He was beautiful to me with his human imperfections—even more so now. What knowledge and understanding he must now possess that mortal man has no access to! Who am I that I should have prevented this heavenly event by one day or even one hour? In my selfishness, I wanted him with me, all the while knowing that this earthly life is only a shadow of heaven's grandeur.

Sometimes in life, we have to love another enough to let that person go. I came to this realization and wrote the above passage several months after my husband had died. I accepted the reality that it wasn't all about me. My spouse's illness and ultimate death were all part of God's plan for *his* life. I had to *let go*. If you have lost a spouse to death, I pray that you will be able to see that loss from an eternal perspective and lovingly *let go*.

You Are His Child

For ye are all the children of God by faith in Christ Jesus.

—Galatians 3:26 (KJV)

Sometimes the concept of being God's child gets lost in the shuffle as we live in this world. We forget who we are. When this happens, it affects how we live our lives, how we feel about ourselves, and how we treat others. Our life experiences and the kind of relationships we have or had with our earthly father can either enhance or skew our perceptions of our *heavenly* Father, but even negative perceptions can be transformed by God's grace.

Imagine how different a day lived in the presence of our loving heavenly Father would be compared to the usual rat race. What do you see? I see a calmer and more fulfilling day. I see myself feeling loved and taking time to show love and care to others. I see myself desiring to talk with my heavenly Father and seeking His direction and help rather than going it alone and ending up feeling stressed and exhausted by the end of the day.

As Christians, we *know* we are God's children, but sometimes we forget what that means. We need the daily reminders God has given us in His Word—reminders that He loves us with a love we don't always understand. It is greater than any love we have ever known on this earth.

We can choose, each day, to consciously seek a relationship with our heavenly Father, to bask in His love for us, and to allow His love to flow through us to others. It's not a childish thing to do; it's what we were created to do. It's who we are!

God's Protection

If you say, "The Lord is my refuge," and you make the Most High your dwelling, no harm will overtake you, no disaster will come near your tent. For He will command His angels concerning you to guard you in all your ways; they will lift you up in their hands, so that you will not strike your foot against a stone.

—Psalm 91:9–12 (NIV)

I don't know about you, but I desire God's protection in my life. I daily pray for it, not only for myself, but also for my family and friends. I often ask God to put a hedge of protection around me, my husband, my children, and my grandchildren. When I travel, I ask Him to put a hedge of protection around my home. When I lived alone after the death of my husband, I nightly asked God to encamp His angels "round about my house" before I went to sleep.

Feeling protected gives us a sense of peace and security. Since we were young, it has been a fundamental need for our sense of well-being. If you grew up with a sense of security in your home, you know what I'm talking about. If you grew up without this sense of protection and security, you also know what I'm talking about. We all want to feel safe, loved, and secure. It's how God made us.

Our heavenly Father asks us to make *Him* our refuge and our dwelling place. He tells us He will command His angels to guard us and even lift us up in their hands to protect us from harm. I am convinced this happens more often than we realize. I've had times when I've been delayed for one reason or another, and my first response was to think of it as a negative experience. Now I think, *Who knows? We may have missed a bad accident by this delay.* No questions are asked. I'm sure you have also had experiences where you sensed you were being protected, haven't you?

These unseen angelic interventions happen all around us! So let's be thankful to our heavenly Father for His protection in our lives as we seek to make *Him* our refuge and our dwelling place.

16

Keeping Our Eyes on God

Our God, will you not judge them? For we have no power
to face this vast army that is attacking us. We do not know
what to do, but our eyes are on you.

—2 Chronicles 20:12 (NIV)

Like the children of Judah, we face battles in our lives. These battles take various forms for each of us. For some, it is an illness. For others, it may be a failed marriage or a financial crisis. It could be the betrayal of a friend or the death of a spouse.

At times, we feel powerless over our circumstances and simply don't know what to do. Our needs seem to be greater than our resources—not enough money, health, or emotional strength. We become acutely aware of our human limitations. So what can we do?

If you're like me, you want to be independent, to analyze a situation, and to come up with your own solutions. Sometimes this works quite well, but at other times, it has the opposite effect. The more I try to fix it, the worse it gets! Sometimes we spin our wheels, thinking we can do something that we're not equipped to do. So what can we do?

We can follow the example of the children of Judah, who said, "Our eyes are on you." We can keep our eyes on God in the midst of our crisis, completely trusting in His power, wisdom, and goodness. We can look to Him and trust Him to fight our battles for us.

In 2 Chronicles 20:15 (NIV), the Lord says, "Do not be afraid or discouraged because of this vast army, for the battle is not yours but God's."

Courage

Have I not commanded you? Be strong and courageous.
Do not be afraid; do not be discouraged, for the Lord
your God will be with you wherever you go.

—Joshua 1:9 (NIV)

I try not to dwell on my time of widowhood too much, but
I reflect on it just enough to glean the lessons it taught
me. I also draw upon that time in my life to share insights
and comfort with those who are now walking the same path.

Courage is one of the lessons I learned. God tells us to be
strong and courageous and not to be afraid or discouraged.
Yet those are the very feelings we experience when we grieve
the death of our mate. So how do we become strong and
courageous in the midst of our circumstances?

Joshua 1:9 gives us the answer. We are told that we can
be strong and courageous because God is with us wherever
we go. Yes, He was with me during the months of my late
husband's hospitalization. He was with me as I watched him

take his last breath. And He was with me each night I cried myself to sleep.

I didn't feel very courageous in those days, but looking back, I can see that I was more courageous than I had ever been in my life. I had not been in a situation before where I had needed to be that strong. I found courage deep inside me that I didn't know was there. I breathed in courage as I walked the long sidewalk into church alone—the same sidewalk I had walked so many times with my husband.

I breathed in courage as I headed home, night after night, to the empty house that used to be filled with warmth, laughter, and conversation. And I breathed extra deeply on those Saturday nights that used to feel content, regardless of the plans, staying home or going out.

I breathed in courage as I opened up to a counselor when I was used to *being* the counselor and the one giving comfort and support rather than needing it. I was acutely aware of taking that deep breath of courage every time I intentionally made an effort to make new friends or try unfamiliar activities.

During my time of widowhood, I learned that Jesus was leading me along the way He had designed just for me. He goes before me and walks alongside me. I am never alone.

I can't expect others to fully understand His ways with me, any more than I understand His dealings with others. He is leading me day by day and moment by moment. I haven't always understood it or been able to see much further than today. But then, it seems that's how it's supposed to be—following His lead day by day.

This goes against my nature. I want to plan it all out, to

organize it, and to see the future. But I have learned that the Lord will give me just enough light for today as He leads me along the path He has for me.

I'm learning to acknowledge Him in all my ways and to listen for His voice, allowing Him to direct my paths. He gently led me through my season of sorrow to my time of new beginnings. Again, I take a deep breath of courage as I look forward to all He has planned for me!

Life

But seek first His kingdom and His righteousness, and all these things will be added to you. So do not worry about tomorrow; for tomorrow will care for itself. Each day has enough trouble of its own.

—Matthew 6:33–34 (NASB)

Life

Life, with its many twists and turns
Seems to take us on paths we do not know.
Adventure, regret, courage, and fear
All mixed together, our heart yearns.

For safety and solace and peace and rest
We search and find, then lose our way.
Difficulties, loss, laughter, and tears
Over and over, we're put to the test.

> Where do we go? What do we do?
> When we've come to the end of ourselves.
> Failure, sadness, weakness, and longing
> All seem to lead us to You.

This life is filled with uncertainties, and each day has its own challenges. So how are we to find stability in the midst of life's uncertainties? Matthew 6 tells us not to worry about tomorrow because it will take care of itself.

But there is more than not being overly concerned or anxious about life. We are also instructed to seek God first and to seek His righteousness. Only then will we learn to trust Him with our lives.

That doesn't mean everything will be perfect, or that we will flutter about in perpetual happiness. But it means we trust Him. When blessings are flowing into our lives, we trust Him! When difficulties are present, we trust Him!

When we come to the end of ourselves, God is still faithful—faithful to love and care for us and to walk with us throughout our days on this earth. He gives us peace and stability in the midst of the inconsistencies of life as we seek Him first.

God Is Good

For the Lord is good; His lovingkindness is everlasting and His faithfulness to all generations.

—Psalm 100:5 (NASB)

The Bible clearly teaches that God is good and does good things. If our focus is on our experiences of pain, hurt, or fear, it is easy to doubt God's goodness. Experience is a subjective teacher. Unless we interpret our experience in the light of what God's Word says, we are in danger of drawing wrong conclusions from it.

I am very grateful for the goodness of God in my life. That doesn't mean everything has always been perfect, but it does mean God is faithful and good. He restores us when we wander, heals us when we are hurting, and loves us with a love too deep to understand.

I have learned that things are not always as they may seem. Our human perspective is often skewed by faulty assumptions and perceptions. We can become discouraged when our expectations are not met. Sometimes we allow our feelings to dictate how we assess a situation. Yet God's wisdom allows certain things for our ultimate good.

It is important for us to balance our feelings and assumptions with God's Word and prayer. We will then be able to trust in God's goodness and mercy, knowing He is with us regardless of our circumstances. With confidence, we can say, "God is good!"

Strength Made Perfect in Weakness

And he said unto me, "My grace is sufficient for thee: for my strength is made perfect in weakness." Most gladly therefore will I rather glory in my infirmities, that the power of Christ may rest upon me.

—2 Corinthians 12:9 (KJV)

We all like to be strong, look strong, and feel strong. Yet there are times during our lives when we feel anything but strong. As we watch a parent or grandparent age, we are brought to terms with our own potential for frailty.

Aging parents may contemplate the contrast between their younger, stronger years and the way they are now. Some yearn for the simple pleasures that seem to have grown wings and flown away—simple things like driving their cars, going shopping by themselves, or taking an evening stroll around the neighborhood.

Yet God tells us in His Word that His grace is sufficient for us because His strength is made perfect in weakness. In

2 Corinthians 12:9 (KJV), Paul goes a step further by saying that he would gladly consider his infirmities a source of honor "that the power of Christ may rest upon me."

I have a friend who lives this out on a daily basis. Although she has infirmity in her body, her spirit shines forth with the strength and power of Christ. She is an example to me of what this scripture truly means! May God bless each of us with the grace to be an example of His great strength being made perfect in our weakness.

If We Could Only See

For now we see through a glass, darkly; but then face to face: Now I know in part; but then shall I know even as also I am known.

—1 Corinthians 13:12 (KJV)

If We Could Only See

If we could only see
A little further than today
We'd know this life on earth is short
We'd walk a different way.

If we could only see
Inside another's heart
We'd understand his hurt and pain
We'd hug him from the start.

If we could only see
God looking down on us
We'd smile and say, "Good morning Lord …
"In You I put my trust!"

If we could only see
The rainbow after the storm
We'd cease our worry and our care
And rest in His arms so warm.

If we could only see
What heaven is really about
We'd earnestly seek God's face
And turn to Christ without a doubt.

How differently we would live our lives, *if we could only see!* Viewing life from the perspective of eternity is certainly different from the shortsightedness many of us have. Even Christians, who know they have eternal life, often lose sight of their heavenly home.

An eternal view gives us hope in the midst of a fallen world. It changes our priorities, causing us to value people over things and relationships over successes. It reminds us to slow down and be grateful for our blessings and to exchange worry for trust.

Having an eternal view makes us more aware of God's presence and the importance of earnestly seeking His face. It causes us to turn to Jesus and to desire and pray for the salvation of others. Selfishness turns into compassion as we serve and care for those in need. We become kinder and more forgiving to those around us.

I'd like you to ask yourself a few questions:

If I could only see what heaven is really about, what would be different about my life today?

What attitudes would change?

Would I treat people any differently?

What would my relationship with God look like?

May God bless each of our lives as we seek to live with an eternal perspective!

22

Anchor of Our Soul

This hope we have as an anchor of the soul, a *hope* both sure and steadfast and one which enters within the veil, where Jesus has entered as a forerunner for us, having become a high priest forever after the order of Melchizedek.

—Hebrews 6:19–20 (NASB)

"On Christ, the solid rock, I stand. All other ground is sinking sand, all other ground is sinking sand. In every high and stormy gale, my anchor holds within the veil." These lyrics from the hymn "My Hope Is Built on Nothing Less" kept going through my mind, over and over, like a catchy tune that wouldn't stop. So I took some time to think about their meaning.

Hebrews 6:19–20 gives us a background for the meaning of the song. Jesus is the anchor of our soul! He's our solid rock and our hope—sure and steadfast. He is our high priest! In every storm of life, He is the anchor that holds us steady.

But sometimes we try to let other people or things be our anchor instead of trusting fully in Christ. What happens if your husband is your anchor, and he dies? What if you look to your job or finances for security and lose them? How about when our families or friends let us down? What then?

Christ is the only true anchor of our soul. When you put down an anchor that's too small, it doesn't hold, and your ship is tossed in the storm. If Christ is our anchor, we can weather the storms of life because "our anchor holds."

I was in a store and noticed a tattoo of an anchor on a young woman's wrist. Since I had already been giving some thought to the significance of allowing Christ to be my anchor, I asked her if her tattoo had any specific meaning. She said she had just chosen it because it was cute.

This conversation reminded me of all the people who go through life oblivious to what it means to have Christ as the anchor of their soul. They look to other much smaller anchors to help them during life's inevitable storms. Drugs, alcohol, relationships, or money don't give them the security they're seeking. They need a solid rock, a strong anchor. They need a savior. My prayer is that those of us who know Christ will put our hope and trust in Him as our strong anchor and that those who haven't accepted Christ will come to know Him.

23

Sweet Assurance

I know that my redeemer lives, and that in the end he will
stand on the earth. And after my skin has been destroyed,
yet in my flesh I will see God; I myself will see him with
my own eyes—I, and not another. How my heart yearns
within me!

—Job 19:25–27 (NIV)

I just happened to open my Bible to Job 19 during one of my
quiet times. I don't always *just* open my Bible randomly to
read—but sometimes. I was reading, verse after verse, as Job
went into quite a bit of detail about his sorry plight.

On and on it went, one misfortune after another, each
stripping away his dignity—even the little boys mocked him.
This man who had been strong, prosperous, and a pillar in
his community was now at the bottom of the heap. He asked
his friends for pity but received only ridicule and judgment.

Job had lived righteously, helping others. Yet in Job 19:21–
22 (NIV), he said, "for the hand of God has struck me." He

asked his friends, "Why do you pursue me as God does?" Job felt God was angry with him but didn't understand why.

As I continued to read this woesome dialogue, verses twenty-five through twenty-seven jumped out at me. I thought, *Where did this come from?* Job was saying, "I know that my redeemer lives ... I will see God ... How my heart yearns within me!" Amazing! In the midst of all of Job's loss and suffering, he still had the sweet assurance that his Redeemer lives and that he would see Him some day.

What a lesson for us! In times of sorrow, we can still have the assurance that our Savior lives and that we will see Him someday. If you are going through your own season of loss, may Job's example encourage you to lift your eyes heavenward in the sweet assurance of God's love for you.

For a Season

To every *thing there is* a season, and a time to every purpose under the heaven:

—Ecclesiastes 3:1 (KJV)

As nature has its seasons, so do our lives. I look back on an earlier time in my life when I was raising my young children, and it feels as though it were another lifetime. I've often wondered if other people feel that way as well. We take photographs and videos, keep journals, and reminisce with old friends as we come to terms with the reality that everything on this earth is for a season.

If we live long enough, most of us will remember relationships that had a beginning and an end. Maybe it was a time in your life when you were at your peak in your ministry or career. That, too, had a starting point and a time of transition or retirement. Sometimes this peak is viewed as a time when you felt more important or useful. Parents often view their empty nest as a life change that ended the season of feeling needed by their children.

The way we think about past seasons in our lives can greatly affect our current one. Are we looking back with disappointment that we are not still *there* or are we embracing this new time in our lives with a sense of adventure, joy, and thankfulness? As the seasons of nature are different yet each beautiful, each having its own purpose, so are the seasons of our lives.

We can get stuck, wistfully looking back over our shoulder, or we can be fully present in our current experiences, relationships, and challenges. When we invest our energy into making the present the best time of our lives, it prevents comparisons that lead to feelings of disappointment. By all means, be grateful for every past blessing and learn from any mistakes or failures from those early years. These all work together to make us who we are and form our sense of identity.

But don't let any of those memories, positive or negative, overshadow what God has planned for your life now—new relationships to be nurtured, new challenges to meet, and new areas of work or ministry. It could even be a much-needed season of rest and relaxation for you to recreate yourself after a major life experience has left you drained. Whatever season it is, embrace it! It has beauty, and it has purpose!

May God help us as we maneuver through the many transitions of life. May He give us the wisdom to understand that "to everything there is a season and a time for every purpose." May we fully trust Him as He gently leads us through all the seasons of our lives!

Keep on Going

"For I know the plans I have for you," declares the Lord, "plans to prosper you and not to harm you, plans to give you hope and a future."

—Jeremiah 29:11 NIV)

I recently heard a minister say that we can survive anything if we "keep on going." He told us not to put our anchor down in the storm but to keep on going until we get to our destination.

If someone had said those words to me in my early stages of grief, I would have thought, *Until I get where I'm going? I can barely get out of bed in the morning! Where I'm going doesn't even register in my brain right now.*

I am thankful I eventually came to the point of thinking about where I was going. I decided I didn't want to get stuck in debilitating grief. This decision comes at a different time for each person who is experiencing loss. There's no magic formula, no step one or two that you have to follow perfectly, and no rushing it!

At that time, I considered my widowhood as my year of sorrow and deep spiritual growth. I now consider this season of my life as a time of new beginnings and continued spiritual growth. I decided I wanted to live, love, and laugh again. With God's grace and provision, I have been able to emerge from my grief whole and have a blessed life, happy marriage, and a fulfilling purpose.

God has not changed. He is still faithful in His promises to us. So don't put your anchor down in the storm! In other words, don't get stuck in your grief. Keep on going until you get to your destination—the place where you find yourself living, loving, and smiling again.

I pray for each one of you who has weathered the stormy sea of grief. May God give you hope as you keep on going.

The God Who Sees Me

The angel of the Lord found Hagar near a spring in the desert; it was the spring that is beside the road to Shur. And he said, "Hagar, slave of Sarai, where have you come from, and where are you going?"

"I'm running away from my mistress Sarai," she answered.

She gave this name to the Lord who spoke to her: "You are the God who sees me," for she said, "I have now seen the One who sees me."

—Genesis 16:7–8, 13 (NIV)

Have you ever, like Hagar, been in a desperate situation and realized later that God saw you? He was there with you all along, having compassion on you and working behind the scenes to bring blessing into your life.

During the months after my late husband's death, my heart was heavy during a particular holiday. As I cried out to God, I didn't understand what He was doing in my life. Why was I going through this?

Now, several years later, I can still recall the hurt and the pain, but I see a different scenario than I saw at that time. God saw me! He was there with me, and He had compassion on me. I now understand more of what He *was* and *is* doing in my life.

As I recall a recent weekend, relaxing in a quaint mountain town with Eric, I feel so blessed, loved, and cared for. God has blessed me with a loving husband and a peaceful life. The sting of widowhood has been replaced with the warmth of love.

If you are alone, I hope you will realize that God sees your hurts, and He is with you. May you know in your heart that He is already at work behind the scenes to bring blessing into your life. May you be able to say, "You are the God who sees me!"

Reflections on Widowhood

Sing to God, sing in praise of his name, extol him who rides on the clouds; rejoice before him—his name is the Lord … a defender of widows, is God in his holy dwelling.

—Psalm 68:4–5 (NIV)

Although I was a widow for less than two years before I remarried, I was totally immersed in widowhood during that time. I felt its sting, its uncertainty, and its aloneness. I grieved deeply and was acutely aware of my own powerlessness.

As a result, I have a heart for widows. I often pray for them and try to encourage them. I pressed into God during that time and went to a support group and to grief counseling. As a professional counselor, I knew what I needed to do to emerge from my grief whole.

As I looked back over some of my writing during that time, I found the following lines:

I have to figure this out. How to go on with my life

without my mate with me—to go on in dignity, peace, and joy. I have to learn again to be independent while depending on God for my strength, direction, and identity. Going to Him with my hurts, fears, and needs while simultaneously reaching out to others with love, faith, and joy. Allowing God's strength and love to flow through me to others. Looking daily for God's blessings. Looking for ways to be a blessing.

As you can see, I had no desire to *get stuck* in my grief. I wanted to emerge whole so that I could be a blessing to others. I didn't want to wallow in self-pity or hopelessness.

I am grateful to God for gently leading me through my time of widowhood, for teaching me many lessons, and for giving me hope. He has a plan for all of our lives—even in widowhood—and He has a plan for *you*!

28

It's a Very Good Life

O taste and see that the Lord *is* good: blessed *is* the man *that* trusteth in Him.

—Psalm 34:8 (KJV)

I've been through some difficult experiences in my life—some of them were of my own making and others were not. I'm certain, many of you could say the same thing. Yet I can honestly say, "It's a very good life!"

My heart is full of contentment and peace as I reflect on prayers answered, hopes fulfilled, and love shared. Relationships with children and grandchildren are a constant source of satisfaction. The ever-deepening love shared with my husband is a delight, and I am still in awe of God's love for me. It's a very good life!

Memories are sweet, and dreams are exciting, but I have chosen to live in the present because that is where life is truly experienced—listening to my husband play the piano or playing on the floor with my grandson. What could be better than the simple pleasures of life? What more could we ask for?

In our youth, we seem to find it difficult to be content. We're always looking for the next success or purchase to make us happy. We try to mold life around us and around our perception of what it *should* be. We try to change circumstances and even people to fit our liking. As we grow older and hopefully wiser, we are able to let go of this pursuit and simply enjoy life.

We begin to clearly see that God is in control. We learn to trust Him and His best for us. Only then are we able to relax enough to appreciate all that makes up *our* life—beautiful relationships, family, friends, and home. As I have discovered, we are then able to say, "It's a very good life!"

29

It's Springtime at Last!

...weeping may endure for a night, but joy cometh *in the morning.*

—Psalm 30:5b (KJV)

Have you ever felt like that? "It's springtime at last!" I was glad to hear those words. It was the first day of spring. In Florida, the winter hasn't been that bad, of course, but I'm still looking forward to the blessings of spring—mild temperatures, colorful flowers, and the freshness and sense of newness all around! It is truly a time of new beginnings, fresh starts, and beauty—a time of refreshing.

A few years ago, I said yes to a new beginning and a fresh start. My husband loves to tell the story of how he asked me to kneel down by the hassock in my living room to pray with him. At the end of our prayer time, he asked me two questions. "Stephanie, will you marry me?" *and* "Will you serve God with me?" Having been a missionary for over thirty-five years, he didn't want to be like a traveling salesman. He wanted his wife to join him in the mission. My answers were, "Yes," *and* "Yes!"

This has been a "springtime" in our lives, after having gone through the illness and death of our mates. As the psalmist says, "Weeping may endure for a night, but joy comes in the morning." Although grief can last many nights, months, or even years—joy will be restored. This may be hard for you to grasp if you are grieving the loss of a spouse or a family member. But a brighter day is coming as you press into God and trust Him with your future. You will be able to say, "It's springtime at last!"

PART 2

List of 44

Delight yourself in the Lord; And He will give you the desires of your heart.

—Psalm 37:4 (NASB)

Months after my husband had moved to heaven, I spoke to a friend who shared with me how she had asked God for specific traits in the man she would eventually marry. I began to think I needed to do the same. Even though I wasn't ready to start dating just yet, I started working on my list. Before the evening was over, I came up with forty-four specific traits I wanted in the man who would be my husband. I made this list into a prayer:

Dear God,

These are the traits I want in a husband. I pray that when your timing is right, you would put him right in front of me—no seeking on my part. And I ask that we would both know beyond a shadow of a doubt that You are bringing us together. Give us a great love for each other that we might bring glory to You. Amen.

I won't go into my entire list of forty-four traits, but I'll hit some of the highlights. I wanted him to be close to my age and to value living a responsible and healthy lifestyle. I asked that he would love God with all his heart, be a dedicated Christian, and love God's Word. I wanted him to be willing to attend a church that was comfortable for both of us and to have a heart for ministry to others.

I asked that he would be emotionally mature, kind, patient, and loving—basically that he would have the fruit of the Spirit. I wanted him to be a good communicator, willing to talk about his feelings, and a good listener. It was important to me for him to have a good sense of humor and to make me laugh every day. Along with that, I didn't want him to have any anger or control issues, and he needed to be able to resolve conflicts in a healthy, respectful manner.

I asked that he be supportive of me and not try to change me. I wanted him to accept my children and grandchildren and have a special heart and acceptance for my grandson, who has autism. Also, it was important for him to agree with the concept of adding to each other's life rather than taking away.

I asked for us to have chemistry, even at our age, and for him to be affectionate. It was also my desire for him to enjoy traveling and to appreciate nature. I wanted us to have a servant's heart toward each other, to care for each other when needed, and to lovingly and mutually serve each other.

These are some of the main points on my "List of 44." They were my requests in prayer that evening, and I am happy to say that God gave me the desires of my heart! I pray that you receive the desires of your heart as you prayerfully seek God's direction in your life and as you delight yourself in the Lord.

Honoring God in Our Marriage

> Husbands, love your wives, just as Christ loved the church
> and gave himself up for her ... However, each one of you
> also must love his wife as he loves himself, and the wife
> must respect her husband.

> —Ephesians 5:25, 33 (NIV)

What if God's wisdom on marriage was crystal clear to us from the start? Maybe there would be more happiness and fewer broken homes. Unfortunately, most of us have to glean our clarity on marriage from our own failures and mistakes and learn the hard way.

What if the purpose of marriage is to honor God? That doesn't sound like the first thought that comes to mind when we're contemplating marriage. It's more like love, physical intimacy, companionship, family, and growing old together, right? These are all legitimate and healthy aspects of marriage—but there's more! Marriage provides a pathway for deep spiritual growth as we choose to honor God in our relationship with our husband or wife.

Having a servant's heart toward each other is one way to not only honor the other person but to also honor God in your marriage. There's nothing more beautiful than to see a man and a woman gladly serving each other, when it is mutual and not one-sided. When it's about more than the human relationship, it goes higher in purpose to please and honor God. Lovingly serving each other will grow your love, not diminish it. It will enrich you, not diminish you.

Marriage is the most intimate opportunity you will ever have in your life to minister to another human being. It is also the most important! But we can't do it on our own. Our personal relationship with Christ is the foundation upon which we build a loving relationship with our spouse. If we lean on our own inclinations, we will often fail because we can be selfish and insensitive at times (human nature). But in Christ, we have a higher calling—to love each other. Love that ministers, involves the extension of one's self for the spiritual growth of the other.

Husbands and wives need to love and respect each other. This is not negotiable. Every word, action, and motivation should flow from a deep respect for the other person. It's a beautiful thing when both husband and wife seek to be an extension of God's love to each other. This honors your mate, your marriage, and God!

I will always remember the words spoken by the minister at my wedding. He shared that the more a man has of God, the more he is able to love his wife. The more a wife has of God, the more she is able to love her husband. May we continually keep our hearts open to God's love as we endeavor to honor Him in our marriage.

Wedding Day Anticipation

My beloved is mine and I am his.

—Song of Songs 2:16 (NIV)

A week before my wedding, I wrote about my anticipation of that day:

My heart is joyful as I anticipate our wedding day! I look forward to our commitment celebration with friends and family, in the presence of God.

I was telling one of my dear friends, today, that I feel right in the center of God's will. No doubts! At peace! Happy and looking forward to our life together.

I am amazed at God's providence in bringing us together at this time in our lives. It's been a beautiful experience for both of us, and I can't tell you how many of our friends have shared with us that they see God's hand in this. Many have told us they see our union as an answer to their prayers. Although I haven't needed confirmation from others, I have received that confirmation over and over again.

In one week, we become one in God's eyes. We already know we are stronger together than apart. We already share a deep spiritual bond. We pray for each other and for each other's family and friends.

One thing that has impressed me from the beginning is that he prays. I mean, this man *really* prays! And that has blessed my life. We have already seen answers to prayers together.

We've also discovered we're a good team, taking care of business and getting things done. We have fun together and he makes me laugh every day. That is something I specifically asked God for. In fact, it's a joke with my family that I ended up with a list of forty-four items when I was describing to God what kind of man I would like Him to send my way.

I am mature enough to know that life isn't perfect and neither of us is perfect, but with God's help and grace and our mutual commitment to honor God in our marriage, I believe we will have a happy and fulfilling life together.

None of us know what the future holds here on this earth. We walk by faith, trusting God to lead us and to give us wisdom for each day—trusting Him to give us enough light for that day's journey.

Love Takes Courage

Be strong and courageous.

—Deuteronomy 31:6a (NASB)

L ove takes courage! You may ask, "Why? Isn't love supposed to be beautiful and fulfilling?" Yes, and it is, but it also holds the possibility of hurt. Ouch!

To truly love someone, whether it is your spouse, your child, or your friend, requires vulnerability, and vulnerability can be a scary thing. Your heart and soul are laid bare in order to be close to the one you love. In most situations, the recipients of your love will also become vulnerable to you and genuinely share who they are. They will reciprocate your love.

There is always the potential risk of rejection, betrayal, or being taken for granted. People may get upset with you for one reason or another, gossip about you, or simply ignore you. Then what? Do you just close up and retreat or do you keep on opening your heart to love?

Christ is our example of courageous love. He did not retreat or close His heart. He lived out His love for us in the face of rejection and betrayal. Today, many still ignore Him and choose to reject Him, yet He lovingly waits with outstretched arms!

May you be courageous as you open your heart to others. The rewards far outweigh the risks of vulnerability. I hope you take the opportunity to let those you love know just how much they mean to you—with your *words* and *actions*. You may be pleasantly surprised at their response.

All Is Not As It Seems

...be ye therefore wise as serpents, and harmless as doves.

—Matthew 10:16b (KJV)

I want to write on this topic because I have seen far too many Christians, both men and women, hurt and devastated. I don't know any other way to say it but straight out—people, including those who profess to be Christians, are not always as they seem. So don't be paranoid but instead, be aware!

I have seen people deeply hurt after marrying someone they considered to be a *good* Christian. I have counseled numerous couples in my private practice who realized, too late, that the person they married was not the same person they had dated.

I'm not talking about the little things. We're all on our best behavior during the courtship phase, and some things simply relax after marriage. This is perfectly normal and to be expected. I'm talking about something deeper, something very serious and dysfunctional, and something that will drastically affect the quality and success of your marriage relationship. The frightening thing about it is most people don't have a clue until *after* the wedding!

This does not include the cases where red flags are waving furiously, but the other person is so insecure and needy they deny or ignore the warnings and walk right into the marriage anyway. In that situation, you have two dysfunctional people trying to make a marriage work.

Then there is the vulnerable person who is easily deceived during the dating process. They may be basically healthy but are experiencing some vulnerability due to their life circumstances. Some widows or widowers can fall into this category. They may have been treated well by their former spouse and mistakenly assume their new love interest will possess the same positive qualities they were accustomed to—big mistake!

It is also naïve to assume that a man or a woman will be a good marriage partner just because they are a *good* Christian. All of us are at different levels of maturity, emotionally and spiritually. Don't make the mistake of assuming people are mature Christians just because they have been in church for twenty years. Be aware that emotional maturity is not always based on a person's biological age. Unfortunately, it is sometimes closer to their shoe size.

I know I sound a bit cynical here, but my goal is not for you to become jaded in your thinking but that you will be realistic and use wisdom. The old saying, "An ounce of prevention is worth a pound of cure," is an understatement when it comes to these matters.

The types of dysfunction I am referring to can, at

first, seem quite subtle or harmless. A small slight is easily overlooked, but deep anger and control issues rear their ugly heads quickly after the nuptials (sometimes as quickly as the honeymoon). Other unresolved generational family dysfunctions such as intimacy issues or personality disorders, are impossible for the person to cover up indefinitely. Even if counseling is sought, it will be ineffective unless both partners are *willing* to take an honest look at themselves.

Many people have built up layer upon layer of defenses over the years. Instead of acknowledging their own issues, they choose to blame their mates or to project problems onto others. In other words, they need intensive, long-term therapy just to get to the place of being able to deal with marital issues in a healthy manner.

The gift of marriage between two mature, healthy people who love God with all their heart is a beautiful thing. May you carefully and sincerely seek God's wisdom and direction as you make one of the most important decisions of your life.

Good Communication in Marriage

A word fitly spoken *is like* apples of gold in pictures of silver.

—Proverbs 25:11 (KJV)

As a marriage therapist, I have found communication to be at the top of the list of reasons couples seek marriage counseling. If you want a strong marriage, you can't ignore the importance of good communication. Do you want more happiness in your marriage? How about deeper intimacy? Communication is the place to start if you want to enhance the quality of your relationship.

Good communication in marriage is healthy for your emotional well-being and increases your potential for personal and relational growth. It's good for your health because it allows you to deal with conflict and stress in ways that foster intimacy rather than isolation. Good communication helps you feel close to your partner and allows you to give and receive love. The bottom line is—it's just *good* for you!

During my years of practice, I discovered several important distinctions in the communication patterns of happily versus unhappily married couples. First of all, they prioritize their lives in ways that allow them time to be together and time to communicate with each other in a meaningful way. In other words, their relationship is a priority to them, and they are involved in each other's lives! They also discuss a broader range of topics and experience greater satisfaction as they share their individual interests and endeavors with each other.

Strong couples keep their lines of communication open. Too much distance can occur if a husband and wife are not talking enough. This happens if one partner is silent too often, closes the other out of his or her private world, or gets too busy to stay emotionally close. Resentment can result when this distance is perceived by one or both spouses.

Successful couples recognize that good communication is necessary to maintain a healthy, satisfying marriage and to foster growth in their relationship. They thrive in an atmosphere of openness and are able to communicate a genuine sense of care and concern for each other. These couples work at developing appropriate communication patterns and show more sensitivity to each other's feelings than unhappily married couples. Partners grow in trust as they experience a heightened sense of emotional security and relational stability in this type of environment.

No one is perfect in this area. We are all still growing, regardless of our age or how long we've been married. But none of us can afford to take lightly the importance of developing good communication in our marriage. The strength and success of our relationship depends on it! Our happiness and sense of well-being are affected by it! And the person we, in the presence of God, have committed to love, honor, and cherish *deserves* it!

An Intimate Marriage

For this reason a man shall leave his father and his mother,
and be joined to his wife; and they shall become one flesh.

—Genesis 2:24 (NASB)

In God's eyes, we have become one flesh as husband and wife. This is very intimate, yet many married couples struggle with intimacy issues, both physically and emotionally. As a marriage therapist for many years, I saw the strong connection between the emotional and the physical.

I've found that our communication patterns play a big role in our ability to achieve and maintain genuine intimacy in our marriage relationship. This intimacy requires a high level of vulnerability with our partner, and let's face it, that can be scary unless you totally trust each other!

We tend to be *ourselves* with people who will not use their knowledge of who we are against us. Most of us start out in our marriage with this level of trust, but unfortunately, the way we communicate with each other can cause us to close up, become resentful, or become defensive. We stop being vulnerable, and the quality of our intimacy suffers.

You are probably wondering how to prevent this dynamic from taking place in your own marriage, right? First of all, it's important to be aware of the communication patterns that foster intimacy and those that destroy it. We all know that negativity, harshness, and criticism are not conducive to a close relationship, but how about busyness, lack of eye contact, and forgetting to compliment each other?

Maybe you're not attentive when your partner is speaking to you. After all, they pick the worst time to interrupt your TV program! There's also the issue of only talking about facts or the ideas of others instead of opening up about your own feelings or tuning into how your mate feels emotionally.

Instead of taking your spouse for granted, how about using words of encouragement, validation, and empathy to express your love? Why not give gentle touch and eye contact to let them know they have your undivided attention and you understand what is being said. Being kind and respectful in all of your interactions helps both of you risk being vulnerable with each other. Spending uninterrupted time together may be one of the best things you can do for your marriage.

Building intimacy in your marriage takes time and attention, but the rewards are well worth your efforts! Think of it as an investment you are making in each other and in your life together. May God bless you as you enjoy the many benefits of an intimate marriage!

37

The Beauty of a Gentle and Quiet Spirit

Wives, in the same way submit yourselves to your own husbands so that, if any of them do not believe the word, they may be won over without words by the behavior of their wives, when they see the purity and reverence of your lives. Your beauty should not come from outward adornment ... Rather, it should be that of your inner self, the unfading beauty of a gentle and quiet spirit, which is of great worth in God's sight.

—1 Peter 3:1–4 (NIV)

If you are a Christian wife, I want to encourage you to allow your beauty to shine from within. We all want to have a beautiful physical appearance. We want our husbands to find us desirable and to see us as beautiful, but let's not stop at nurturing only the unique physical beauty we each possess. Let's also nurture the "unfading beauty of a gentle and quiet spirit."

God's Word tells us that even the unbelieving husband will be won to Christ without words when he sees the pure and reverent behavior of his wife. I want to emphasize the *without words* part of this scripture. Too often, as women, we want to talk about everything that crosses our mind, but sometimes, we just need to be quiet. That's right—not say a word about something that might be bothering us.

You may think this is contradictory to all that we have been taught about healthy communication in marriage. But I have learned, sometimes the hard way, that it is best not to bring up an issue until I have first prayed about it *from the inside out*, poured my heart out to God, given it to God, waited on Him for an answer, and God has poured His love and grace all over the situation.

Wait until you have clear direction from God's Word— until you understand what you need to learn from the situation and how you can grow through it. At times, that direction may be to simply *let go* and let God fight your battles for you. Let Him change the person or situation as only He can. Then we, as Christian wives, will continue to dazzle our husbands with our beauty—with the beauty of a gentle and quiet spirit!

38

Anger in Marriage

My dear brothers and sisters, take note of this: everyone should be quick to listen, slow to speak and slow to become angry, because human anger does not produce the righteousness that God desires.

—James 1:19–20 (NIV)

It's unfortunate to see the relational damage that results when couples fail to learn how to communicate appropriately around anger and conflict. Emotional distance is one of the most common symptoms of deep anger and results in a refusal or lack of ability to allow others to get close. When this occurs, a person's ability to give and receive love is blocked and attempts at developing a satisfying marital relationship are hindered.

Listening is a major part of the communication process. Poor listening leads to misunderstandings and arguments, but good listening leads couples toward greater levels of intimacy and satisfaction.

Some couples find they have become polarized with no middle ground. Others withdraw emotionally from the relationship in an effort to protect their bruised egos. When this happens, trust is damaged and hope is drained. In extreme cases, an abusive cycle is set in place, which results in low self-esteem and depression.

There are differences in how men and women communicate when they are angry or upset. Some studies suggest that a woman tends to blame a man and may sound critical or resentful when she feels a surge of negative emotions. It can be difficult for her to communicate in an accepting, trusting manner during these times of conflict.

When a man becomes upset, he may become judgmental of a woman and her feelings. In his anger or hurt, he may not remember that she is sensitive and vulnerable, may forget her needs, and may come across as uncaring. When he feels a surge of negative emotion, it may be hard for him to speak to her in a respectful and caring manner.

During these times, when talking doesn't work, it's best for couples to take a cool down break or to write out their feelings in the form of a letter to their spouse. It's not necessary, and often not advisable, to give the letter to your mate. The activity is valuable, in the sense that it prevents escalation and allows you to process your own feelings in order to be able to express them in a more rational manner.

As Christians, God's Word calls us to a higher standard. Although we struggle with the weaknesses of our human nature, we can choose patience rather than irritation, love rather than anger, and a gentle spirit instead of harshness.

Then we can experience the kind of marriage God intends for us to have.

Pure acceptance, knowing we have each other's back, and knowing we are enjoyed for who we are instead of someone trying to change us—these are the subtle things that matter! Feeling safe, emotionally and physically, knowing we won't be treated poorly just because someone had a bad day, not having fear of the other person's anger, and not being taken advantage of makes for an environment where defenses are rarely needed.

That's when you can relax and be yourself, where you get a small taste of how God loves you through the love of your mate. May we all learn to be "quick to listen, slow to speak and slow to become angry."

39

Leaving and Cleaving

For this reason a man shall leave his father and his mother,
and be joined to his wife; and they shall become one flesh.

—Genesis 2:24 (NASB)

I just read a devotional about the necessity of making your relationship with your mate the primary relationship after marriage. In other words, leave and cleave. This usually involves couples leaving parents, but in marriage later in life, it can also mean leaving children and even grandchildren.

A minister told his story about how difficult it can be when a young couple moves away from their families to start their ministry. This also came full circle for him as he became the parent waving good-bye to his daughter and her husband as they left to begin their own ministry.

Although the process of leaving and cleaving is difficult, it is absolutely essential for a successful marriage. You cannot truly bond emotionally with your mate if your primary emotional attachment is with another person—parents, children, grandchildren, or even a deceased spouse.

Your relationship with your family does not stop but simply *transitions,* as you and your mate become *one.* This is not only up to you, but it is also important for family members to give their blessing on your union and to do some *letting go.*

When I remarried later in life after the death of my husband, I saw firsthand how challenging it could be for families to make this transition. Since I married a missionary, I not only chose to leave and cleave to my husband but also to join him in his life's work. This involved overseas travel and more travel when in the states. During this time, I kept reaching out, letting my family members know they were still loved and important in my life. They soon realized they had not lost me but had gained a wonderful addition to our family.

May God bless each of you as you put into practice this key principle of biblical marriage. Leave and cleave!

Love

Love is patient, love is kind *and* is not jealous; love does not brag *and* is not arrogant, does not seek its own, is not provoked, does not take into account a wrong *suffered*, does not rejoice in unrighteousness, but rejoices with the truth; bears all things, believes all things, hopes all things, endures all things. Love never fails.

—1 Corinthians 13:4–8 (NASB)

This verse is utilized in many wedding ceremonies, yet it seems to be easily forgotten as couples settle into married life. Some struggle with various parts of this admonition to genuinely love one another.

You may ask, "How can anyone live up to this high standard?" The key is to allow God's love to flow through you to your spouse. The Bible teaches that God is love. As His Spirit lives within you, you will able to love others. Yet many Christians still fall short, make mistakes, and revert to selfishness. Don't give up! Keep trying no matter how many times you fail.

Why is this so difficult for some people? Our level of emotional maturity affects how reactive we are. This reactivity usually looks more like selfishness than love. When a person is overly reactive, he will lash out at his partner over minor irritations. Kindness takes a backseat to unbecoming behavior.

Unmanaged stress levels play a role in impatient behavior—behavior that does not show proper respect to others. How many times has a husband or wife been hurt by the thoughtless words of his or her partner? Instead of taking your stress and frustration out on each other, be mature enough to manage your stressors in a healthy way. If you have been treated unfairly at work, don't come home and yell at your husband or wife. Instead, look to each other for love and support.

Some people simply have low self-esteem and feel insecure. If their spouse succeeds, instead of being happy for them, they become jealous. Instead of lovingly encouraging each other, they tear each other down. In counseling, we call it *leveling*. It means trying to bring someone down to your level so that you can feel better about yourself, which is just the opposite of love.

The sad part about all of this is that couples miss out on so much happiness and peace when they allow themselves to slip into unloving behaviors. Relationship damage and distance result when these types of behaviors become the norm. I pray that each of you will endeavor to choose loving behaviors and words that will build each other up, enhance your marriage, and honor God.

Newlyweds

"A new command I give you: Love one another."

—John 13:34a (NIV)

We're still newlyweds. I have to say, I'm even more in love with this man than ever. Sometimes I tell him, "I don't know how it's possible, but I love you more today than I did yesterday!"

An older couple came up to us after a meeting where Eric had shared our story. They told us how God had also brought them together after they had both lost their mates to death. The woman had a big smile on her face and a twinkle in her eye as she said, "You know, we've been married over twenty years, and it still feels like it was just yesterday!"

As Eric and I walked arm in arm to our car, I said, "Maybe we'll get to feel like newlyweds for the rest of our lives, just like that couple." His reply was, "Why not?"

I hope you have many happy days and years together celebrating the gift of love God has given you. Be thankful for each other. Love and cherish each other. Take time to enjoy sunsets together—take a walk, have a talk. Just have fun! Who knows, maybe all of us can feel like newlyweds for the rest of our lives together. Why not?

Love in Action

Dear children, let us not love with words or speech but with actions and in truth.

—1 John 3:18 (NIV)

I have heard speakers say that love is not a feeling but an action. I tend to disagree with this statement. I believe it is both! Yet love can be put into action even when the feeling is not present. We can choose to love each other, *and* we can choose loving behaviors toward each other. Then feelings of love will follow.

If you have loving feelings toward a person, most likely, your behavior will be loving. The feelings and the behaviors match up. But how do you get this congruency when you're not feeling very loving toward your husband or wife? Maybe you don't even think you *like* your spouse right now. You may dig your heels in and say, "I'm not going to fake it. I'm not going to act loving if I don't feel it."

Over and over in marriage counseling sessions, I have

told couples to "fake it 'til you make it." In other words, choose loving actions toward your mate, even if you're not feeling the love right now. The feelings will follow. Those who took this challenge were happy to report that their feelings of love began to grow—their feelings began to match their behaviors.

As God's Word teaches us, let's not just say we love each other but show it by our actions. May your marriage be enriched by the flow of positive feelings, which will follow your loving behaviors—as you put love in action!

A House Divided

If a house is divided against itself, that house cannot stand.

—Mark 3:25 (NIV)

One of the most heartbreaking things about being a marriage therapist is to literally see a house divided against itself. Although this is not always the case, it is prevalent in the initial stages of therapy. Couples come into my office pointing fingers of blame at each other in hurt and anger. For any number of reasons, they are divided.

Other couples enter therapy in a genuine effort to become aware of their own blind spots and to take responsibility for their roles in the marital difficulties. They are teachable and desire to change their own unproductive behaviors. They are not "divided" against each other but instead, realize they are on the same team, with the mutual goal of improving their relationship. Both partners are open to personal and relational growth. They realize that genuine change can only take place if each person takes responsibility rather than focusing on changing the other.

I can't help but think about all the couples who never enter a therapist's office but live out their married lives in a house that is divided. The children in these households often pay the price of not having a strong sense of security. They are frequently triangled into the conflict, sometimes even feeling they have to choose sides. And a child may be overly focused on as parents compensate for their lack of closeness with each other.

It is my hope that your house will not be divided against itself. May you seek to have a strong foundation by living in harmony with each other and building each other up. If you do encounter conflicts, seek to resolve them in a manner that will draw you closer together rather than tear you apart.

44

Careless Words

But I tell you that every careless word that people speak,
they shall give an accounting for it in the day of judgment.

—Matthew 12:36 (NASB)

Words are too powerful to be treated carelessly! The Bible teaches us that we alone are fully accountable for every word we speak, yet this is often taken lightly. Words can be used for good or for evil and for healing or for wounding. It's our choice.

How many times has a husband or wife been deeply wounded by a mate's careless words? How much relationship damage has occurred when words of criticism or complaining are thrown carelessly about in day-to-day conversation? If you look at the number of divorces in our world today, you may get an idea of how to answer these questions. People are hurting, relationships are suffering, and homes are being broken. It is time for us to be more responsible with our words.

After counseling couples for three decades, I see a strong correlation between careless words and marital satisfaction. When I have been able to help couples see this destructive pattern in their communication, they begin to be more self-aware and less reactive. They start *choosing* more appropriate words to express themselves rather than spouting off whatever comes to mind. They become more accountable in their relationships and experience greater marital satisfaction as a result.

May all of us realize the power of our words to either hurt or heal, build up or tear down. May we take full responsibility for every word we speak as we endeavor to have a satisfying and fulfilling marriage.

Idols of the Heart

Do not be idolaters, as some of them were; as it is written,
"THE PEOPLE SAT DOWN TO EAT AND DRINK,
AND STOOD UP TO PLAY."

—1 Corinthians 10:7 (NASB)

I attended a women's conference with one of my good friends. The theme was, "Idols of the Heart." I always try to have an open mind and heart when I go to something like this. Often, the message is something I think I already know about, but I've learned to dig deeper to see what God has in mind for me.

As women, we are prone to deeply value our relationships. It's how God wired us! With that said, if we're not careful, our relationships can also become idols of our heart. This doesn't mean we have to devalue our relationships, but it does mean that we keep Christ in His proper place in our heart—actually, on the throne.

A woman doesn't purposely wake up and tell herself that her husband, grandchildren, or friends are going to replace Jesus on the throne of her heart that particular day. But in reality, that is exactly what we do, no matter how unintentional it may be. Some of us simply sit down to eat and drink and stand up to play, day after day, without giving our full devotion to God. Our busyness, pleasure, and comfort become our idols.

In contrast, Luke 10:27 (NASB) shows us what it looks like to have our lives and relationships in balance with our devotion to God. Jesus answered, "Love the Lord your God with all your heart and with all your soul and with all your strength and with all your mind;" and, "Love your neighbor as yourself." We each have to determine what this means to us personally. There is no magic formula for living out this admonition. It's a matter of the heart!

46

Marriage Preparation

It is a trap to dedicate something rashly and only later to consider one's vows.

—Proverbs 20:25 (NIV)

I can count only a handful of couples I saw for *premarital* counseling during the three decades I practiced as a marriage and family therapist. But those I counseled for *marital* problems are too numerous to remember. I think we have it backward. Most couples spend more time planning their wedding ceremony than they invest in preparing for marriage.

With soaring divorce rates, it would serve us well to take an honest look at ourselves before we make one of the most important decisions of our life. First of all, where are you? You may wonder what I mean by this question, but where are you in your maturity level? Where are you in your faith? Where are you in your understanding of what a healthy relationship looks like? Are you ready to take an honest inventory of yourself before attempting to answer these questions?

Maturity and chronological age do not always match. We've all seen examples of this. You may know a young adult who is exceptionally mature for his age, and we have all seen an older adult who comes across as very immature. How mature are you? Do you take responsibility for your actions and for your life? Can you deal with anger appropriately? Do you know how to analyze a situation and to make a wise decision? Don't try to choose a marriage partner if you can't answer a resounding *yes* to these questions.

Some choose a marriage partner during a time in life when they aren't necessarily walking close to God. Later, they become disillusioned with a mate who doesn't value their faith or attend church with them. What were they thinking? How much better it is to be in a place where you are praying and listening to God's voice of direction in your life *before* choosing your mate.

Not everyone understands what it takes to have a healthy marriage relationship. Their attitudes and expectations can be skewed by faulty role models, family dysfunction, and negative life experiences. Be sure you understand the basics before you embark on this venture. Without a good foundation, marriages can crumble beneath the weight of everyday stress. Even if you think you have a good handle on healthy relationship dynamics, don't make the mistake of assuming the other person does as well.

Marriage is a beautiful gift from God and should not be entered into rashly. Our choice of a mate, our commitment, and our marriage vows must be taken seriously. May God bless you as you seek His guidance in your marriage preparation.

Examples in Love

Dear children, let us not love with words or speech but with actions and in truth.

—1 John 3:18 (NIV)

I heard about a young woman in Europe who observed an older couple waiting for the subway. She described them as walking hand in hand, and as they stopped, the man lovingly looked at his wife, as if she was the only woman in the world. He said to her, "You are still beautiful!" The young woman telling the story began to cry and look at the ground so as not to stare at them. She said that her heart was touched because what they were living was what she had dreamed of. She exclaimed, "Love still exists, folks! That's why there is an older couple—to remind us that it is more important than anything else to have someone who loves you unconditionally, will still take your hand, and will tell you how beautiful you are! Thank you to those who are examples in love!"

All of us, as Christians, are called to be examples in love with Christ as our highest example. Older married couples are in a unique position to be examples in love to the younger generation. What a privilege it is to pass on the wisdom of our life experiences through our loving behaviors toward each other.

It has always disturbed me to see an older man or woman being rude and disrespectful to his or her mate. How hurtful that has to be for the other person, who started out with great hope for a loving marriage. If it is the woman being treated shabbily, I see her downcast face as she quietly tries to hide from the obvious disapproval of her husband. If it is a wife carelessly showing disrespect, I see her husband's countenance drop as he braces himself for the attack of the one person who should hold him in highest esteem. What a dark contrast this is to the story of the older couple waiting for the subway.

May we, as older couples, be aware of the influence we have on the younger generation. Let's not take away their hope but instead, by our loving behaviors, assure them love still exists. May God's love shine through us as we continue to be their examples in love!

Protect Her Heart

Husbands, in the same way be considerate as you live with your wives, and treat them with respect as the weaker partner and as heirs with you of the gracious gift of life, so that nothing will hinder your prayers.

—1 Peter 3:7 (NIV)

If you are a husband, I want to encourage you to protect your wife's heart. Shelter her from harm and be her buffer in this world. Always remember that a woman's heart is tender and vulnerable, as it must be for her to love you deeply and intimately.

Be gentle with her and not harsh. Care about her hurts and count it a privilege for her to trust your love enough to bring those hurts to you. She feels deeply because she loves deeply. Don't change who she is with your anger, neglect, or foolishness.

Set boundaries around your relationship with her. She is your wife, your prize, and your gift from God. Don't allow the world to intrude where it should not intrude. Cherish your time together and keep other friendships in their proper perspective. Seek her out as your best friend rather than giving your attention to other women. Seek her admiration rather than that of others.

Her heart yearns for closeness with her husband. Yet, that closeness is only possible through openness and vulnerability. Cherish your closeness with her—as you protect her heart!

Excellence

Then this Daniel was preferred above the presidents and princes, because an excellent spirit *was* in him; and the king thought to set him over the whole realm.

—Daniel 6:3 (KJV)

I spoke to a group of young women at a Christian training event. The topic was, "What Traits Are Important to You in a Person You Would Date or Marry?" Talk about high standards! This group raised the bar. They weren't looking for perfection, but they were certainly expecting *excellence*, and why not?

I was pleased to see young women thinking highly enough of themselves not to settle for a mate who wasn't striving for excellence in his personal life and relationship with God. These women had clearly reached a level of maturity that allowed them to differentiate between mediocrity and excellence. They were seeking excellence in their own lives and valued this trait in the man they wanted to date.

Scripture tells us that Daniel became distinguished because an excellent spirit was in him. Our culture places much value on physical appearance and fitness, and these things are important in the right context—when they're balanced with "an excellent spirit." How many times have you noticed a physically attractive person who, upon speaking, lost his or her appeal? Maybe that person was harsh, prideful, or demeaning of others. This is not attractive!

I have often told women, "It's their spirit you end up living with." Our physical bodies change over time but an excellent spirit follows us throughout our lives. If you are considering dating or marriage, I hope you will set your standard high and not settle for less than what God desires for your life. May God bless you in your pursuit of excellence!

50

Respecting Your Husband

However, each one of you also must love his wife as he
loves himself, and the wife must respect her husband.

—Ephesians 5:33 (NIV)

The genuine respect I feel for my husband is actually a
blessing for me. I am thankful that he lives his life in
such a way that elicits my respect.

As scripture admonishes a Christian wife to respect her
husband, it also admonishes her husband to love her. The
two go hand in hand.

It is a great blessing when a wife's respect for her husband
flows freely, as a natural result of his love for her. My husband
and I often wonder why any couple would want to *mess up*
this beautiful dynamic with thoughtless words, anger, or
selfishness. Maybe they haven't experienced it, so they don't
know what they're missing.

I respect my husband's character, his basic decency, and
his love for God. I often describe him to others as a godly

man whose relationship with God affects how he treats me. Again, this is a blessing for me.

I also respect his commitment to being the spiritual leader of our home. When we are home together, he leads in devotional reading and prayer, *every* night. When we are apart due to travel, he leads in devotional reading and prayer, *every* night, by telephone. This blesses me and draws us closer together on all levels.

So I encourage you to be intentional about treating your husband with respect. May you experience the blessing of having a loving *and* respectful marriage.

First Anniversary

The Lord God said, "It is not good for the man to be alone. I will make a helper suitable for him."

—Genesis 2:18 (NIV)

When my husband and I celebrated our first anniversary, I couldn't help but think, *What a beautiful year. What a blessed life.* I can still say that my husband is the most decent, godly, kind, and loving man I know. These were my thoughts about him before our marriage, and he hasn't changed.

I am thankful he hasn't changed. Some men do, you know. They put their best foot forward when they're dating and then settle into being who they really are shortly after the wedding. It's very disappointing to the bride, who entered into her marriage with hope and trust. When confronted about the negative changes, one husband told his wife, "Well, you wouldn't have married me if I had acted like myself." Come on, now, that's not really fair, is it?

Anyway, I'm glad I'm not dealing with those issues. No one is perfect, but when a man genuinely seeks to honor God by loving and honoring his wife, things go much more smoothly. His wife is blessed by his commitment, and she, in turn, blesses her husband with genuine respect and love. It's a win-win situation, and God is honored in the process.

I am thankful for my husband. I respect him on so many levels and love sharing life with him. I'm looking forward to all God has in store for us as we endeavor to honor Him in our marriage.

In Sync

Do not *merely* look out for your own personal interests,
but also for the interests of others.

—Philippians 2:4 (NASB)

A s my husband and I were having lunch together one
day, the thought just came to my mind, and I said
to him, "We're *in sync* aren't we?" He responded, "Yes," in
agreement with my observation.

Our conversation continued as I pointed out that not
all couples are in sync. Why? Maybe because of selfishness,
control issues, or just being out of touch with each other.
From the viewpoint of someone who is very much enjoying
being in sync with her husband, I wish all couples could
experience this as well.

Actually, when I think about it, not only have my husband
and I *adapted* to what is important to the other, we have also
come to enjoy what the other holds dear. My little grandson
is so important to me. Spending time with him is a priority

for me, even in the midst of our busy ministry travels. Eric's work as a missionary is extremely important to him.

In the process of adapting to each other's priorities, we have both fallen in love with the other's passion. Eric loves my little grandson and is always happy to spend quality time with him. I definitely value and enjoy our ministry work and mission trips.

So if you're having trouble getting in sync with your spouse, why not try showing interest in what he or she is interested in? Don't try to compete with or control your spouse's passion but instead, adapt to it. Who knows, in the process, you may discover that it has become your passion as well. May God bless your marriage as you learn to walk in sync!

PART 3

Circle of Love

Be completely humble and gentle: be patient, bearing with one another in love.

—Ephesians 4:2 (NIV)

Do not judge, or you too will be judged.

—Matthew 7:1 (NIV)

I heard a minister say that if someone draws a circle around you to marginalize you or to judge you, just draw a larger circle to include and love that person. This is not usually our first response, is it? Yet, as Christians, we are called to love and not to judge.

Can you think of anyone in your life who has drawn a circle around you—who has judged or criticized you? Just close your eyes and envision yourself drawing a larger circle of love that includes that person. How does that feel—scary, vulnerable, powerful, or satisfying? You may have a mixture of feelings each time you expand your circle of love.

Remember that you are not responsible for how the other person responds to you. Some people become angry with this type of response while others will soften as they see your good heart. Regardless of the outcome, I encourage you to continue to increase your circle of love in response to criticism or judgment.

This also includes people who *you* may be tempted to judge or look down on. Maybe they have too many tattoos or don't dress the way you think they should. Maybe the homeless person is dirty and a bit scary to you. Again, we're not called to judge but to love. You may be surprised at how much of a blessing someone may be to you as that person responds to your caring behavior. Why not give a smile or a kind word as you pass by, rather than going smugly on your way. May God bless you as you humbly, patiently, and kindly enlarge your circle of love.

Kindness

Be kind and compassionate to one another, forgiving each other, just as in Christ God forgave you.

—Ephesians 4:32 (NIV)

Have you ever had someone kindly say this verse to you when you asked for that person's forgiveness because of thoughtless words—words spoken in hurt or anger? I have, and I can honestly say that it made quite an impact on my heart. First of all, it helped me forgive myself, and secondly, it gave me a deeper love and appreciation for that person. It also deepened my desire to be more like Christ.

That's quite an effect for one verse of scripture spoken in kindness. Powerful words! Yet it wasn't just the words themselves but the living out of those words that made such a difference for me. Can we sincerely say these words to those who offend us? Can we genuinely forgive as God, in Christ, forgave us?

What a different world we would live in if we were all kind, tenderhearted, and forgiving to each other. We can't change our whole world or even those around us, but we can change ourselves.

May God strengthen each of us as we continually purpose in our heart to be more like Christ. May we be kind, tenderhearted, and forgiving to one another.

Compassion

Jesus replied and said, "A man was going down from Jerusalem to Jericho, and fell among robbers, and they stripped him and beat him, and went away leaving him half dead. And by chance a priest was going down on that road, and when he saw him, he passed by on the other side. Likewise a Levite also, when he came to the place and saw him, passed by on the other side. But a Samaritan, who was on a journey, came upon him; and when he saw him, he felt compassion, and came to him and bandaged up his wounds, pouring oil and wine on *them*; and he put him on his own beast, and brought him to an inn and took care of him."

—Luke 10:30–34 (NASB)

Compassion! The Samaritan saw the man in need and had compassion on him while the others passed by. They didn't want to be bothered or slowed down. They went so far as to walk on the other side of the street to avoid any connection with him or his desperate situation. I would like us to honestly ask ourselves, which one are we? How compassionate are we to those in need?

Empathy is a key ingredient of compassion. It is our ability to perceive and reflect back what others around us are feeling. Without empathy we are less able to connect to the pain of others.

Maybe you started out being compassionate to others, but you have been beat up by life. Some of us become more compassionate to others after being broken by difficulties in life, but some people do just the opposite. They become bitter and close themselves off from others when they experience hurt.

Those who tend to become more compassionate have pressed into God during their difficult circumstances. They have been humbled by God but are not angry with Him. They learn to trust in His plan for their lives and find hope for their futures.

Researchers have discovered that a lack of empathy shows up in the brain. The anterior insular cortex has been identified as the epicenter of empathy. There may be reduced activity in these regions of the brain in patients who have difficulty perceiving and sympathizing with another person's pain.

We also know that as humans, we feel happier when we help someone. Medical research indicates that our heart rate decreases and the areas of the brain that are linked to pleasure and nurturing light up when we extend ourselves for others. It is believed that compassion not only relaxes the nervous system but also optimizes the body's ability to heal itself.

Although we certainly reap personal benefits from being compassionate toward others, the very nature of compassion requires that our motivation is to sincerely help the other person. The Bible gives us many examples of Jesus having compassion on others, and in Luke 10:37 (NASB), He says to us, "Go and do the same."

I hope each of us will make a conscious effort to be more aware of the needs of others and to do acts of kindness to meet those needs. May we become genuinely compassionate to others as we not only perceive their needs but also reach out our hands in love to help meet those needs.

56

Imitating Christ's Humility

Do nothing out of selfish ambition or vain conceit. Rather, in humility value others above yourselves, not looking to your own interests but each of you to the interests of others. In your relationships with one another, have the same mindset as Christ Jesus.

—Philippians 2:3–5 (NIV)

Isn't that how you get ahead in life—with ambition, confidence, and by looking out for your own interests? If you're living by the world's standards, the answer is yes. But as you know, scripture often runs contrary to our modern philosophies. Yes, ambition, in its proper place, can be a positive personal trait when it doesn't get ahead of seeking God's direction, tending to the important relationships in our lives, or respecting others.

Confidence is a wonderful attribute when it is paired with humility—knowing our gifts come from God to be used for His purposes and for His glory. When we take full credit for our talents or capabilities, we set ourselves up for a fall. God loves us too much to allow us to be overtaken by pride. He has many, many ways to bring us back to humility, and I think you know what I mean! Most of us have had to be humbled at some point or time in our lives.

Christ's example teaches us to look to the interests of others rather than just looking out for ourselves. In other words, don't be selfish! That's easier said than done in a world that calls out to us with every advertisement to indulge and pamper ourselves. In our it's-all-about-me society, helping others takes a back seat.

I've often wondered what the world would be like if we put some of the energy and time we invest working out at our local gym into mowing our elderly neighbor's yard or raking their leaves? I'm not saying it's wrong to take care of ourselves and exercise. I'm just pondering as to what that would look like if we balanced it with meeting the needs of others.

May God help each of us imitate the humility of Christ in our relationships with others. I believe we will find a greater sense of purpose and fulfillment in our lives as we follow His example.

Our Words

For, "Whoever would love life and see good days must keep their tongue from evil and their lips from deceitful speech."

—1 Peter 3:10 (NIV)

Growing up as a Christian, I remember taking the scripture, spoken by Jesus in Matthew 12:36 (NIV), very seriously. The verse says, "But I tell you that everyone will have to give an account on the day of judgment for every empty word they have spoken."

Because of that, I tried not to gossip or slander others. In high school, I remember one of my friends telling me that I was the only person she knew who didn't gossip. I don't say this to build myself up, because I am sure I have fallen short in this area at times.

We live in a world where people are inclined to give their opinions about any topic or person at any place or time. At times, it seems as though we are becoming a society without boundaries, as we peer into the personal lives of those we barely know on social media and share our own lives as well.

As Christians, we are called to a higher standard—a standard so high that we are told by Christ we will give an account for every empty or idle word we have spoken. The word *empty* is described as vain, futile, worthless, or meaningless. The opposite of that would be to speak words full of meaning and purpose—words to build each other up instead of tearing each other down.

The people in my grandparents' generation seemed to speak less and to measure their words more. They lived by the mantra, "If you can't say something good about someone, don't say anything at all." There was an understood code of ethics to preserve the dignity of others. Older persons were spoken to with respect, valued for their wisdom, and treated with dignity.

We can't control the direction of today's society, but as Christians, we can choose to walk a different way. Let's choose a higher standard as we measure our speech and take responsibility for all of our words.

Unlearning the Art of Social Gossip

Do not let any unwholesome talk come out of your mouths, but only what is helpful for building others up according to their needs, that it may benefit those who listen. And do not grieve the Holy Spirit of God, with whom you were sealed for the day of redemption. Get rid of all bitterness, rage, and anger, brawling and slander, along with every form of malice. Be kind and compassionate to one another, forgiving each other, just as in Christ God forgave you.

—Ephesians 4:29–32 (NIV)

Have you ever been in a situation where gossip seemed to be the art of social discourse? I'm not referring to a secular social setting. I'm referring to us—a gathering of Christian friends.

Even though we may not consider ourselves a gossip, it is easy to get drawn into this type of communication in an effort to fit in or be part of the group. After all, we don't have any bitterness in our heart toward the person we're *discussing*. We're just *expressing our opinion*.

But in no uncertain terms, God's Word tells us to "Stop it!" James 1:26 (NIV) tells us, "Those who consider themselves religious and yet do not keep a tight rein on their tongues deceive themselves, and their religion is worthless." Proverbs 10:19 (NASB) says, "When there are many words, transgression is unavoidable, but he who restrains his lips is wise."

So how do we unlearn the bad habit of social gossip? Rather than winking and laughing at this type of conversation, we must start taking responsibility for what comes out of our mouths. We have to begin taking it seriously because God takes it seriously!

You may feel like you're left with nothing to talk about. What then? Ephesians 4:29 (NIV) gives us the answer, "But only what is helpful for building others up according to their needs, that it may benefit those who listen." We are to simply encourage one another. If the person is not present to receive our encouragement, we can pray *for* them rather than gossip *about* them. Be sure not to allow a prayer request to take the form of gossip.

This type of encouragement involves listening to each other closely enough to understand what the other person may need at that point in time. It is staying in the present and being vulnerable enough to let others know us.

You see, it is only in the absence of gossip that this vulnerability can take place because deep down, we will always wonder if the person who is gossiping about someone else will also talk about us when we're not around. It is my prayer that God will bless our efforts as we determine in our heart to unlearn the art of social gossip.

Spiritual Discipline

On the other hand, discipline yourself for the purpose of godliness; for bodily discipline is only of little profit, but godliness is profitable for all things, since it holds promise for the present life and *also* for the *life* to come.

—1 Timothy 4:7b–8 (NASB)

We all want to be physically, emotionally, and mentally strong. We go to great lengths to maintain and increase our physical strength with trips to the gym, protein drinks, and long walks. We see counselors when we need to express and work through our feelings. We read, take classes, or seek new challenges to stay mentally fit.

These efforts are all necessary to live a balanced, healthy life. Yet we sometimes neglect to give the same priority to our spiritual disciplines—prayer, Bible study, Christian fellowship, or ministering to others. We seem to forget we are spiritual beings living in physical bodies. We need to be spiritually disciplined and strong!

New Christians usually receive teaching on this topic. Many times, it will make the difference between growing to be strong, mature Christians or staying weak and immature. Regardless of the length of time we have been following Christ, we all need to make our spiritual growth a priority. None of us *knows it all* or has had so much experience that we can't learn from God's Word or from other Christians.

It is prideful to have these attitudes. We must remain teachable throughout our lives. That is the only way God can truly use us.

Emotional immaturity in an adult can lead to many problems in a person's life. The same is true for spiritual immaturity. The Bible tells us repeatedly that God wants His children to be strong. So let's not neglect the disciplines that build us up spiritually and produce godliness, not only for this life but also for eternity!

There Is More

For what shall it profit a man, if he shall gain the whole world, and lose his own soul?

—Mark 8:36 (KJV)

As I watch our young people grow up, make plans, and follow their dreams, everything within me wants to say it loud enough for them to truly hear, "There is more!" Yes, their success is commendable. Their talents and gifts are absolutely stunning, yet many are empty. "But they don't *look* empty," you may say. "They have friends, a social life, cars, and stylish clothes." They may even have smiles on their faces because these things satisfy—for a season.

But there is more. Many of our young people don't realize what they are missing. They haven't seen it modeled. So how can they seek after something they don't even know exists?

My prayer is that we, as parents, grandparents, aunts, and uncles, will be able to impart the truth to those growing up in our families—the truth that, through Jesus Christ, they can have a relevant, vibrant, personal relationship with their Creator.

This truth is simple, yet it eludes many. It is powerful, but some give it no significance. My prayer is that our young people will see this truth lived out in our own lives and discover that *there is more*!

Our Young People Deserve More

> Hear, my son, your father's instruction and do not forsake
> your mother's teaching; Indeed, they are a graceful wreath
> to your head and ornaments about your neck.
>
> —Proverbs 1:8–9 (NASB)

When I say our young people deserve more, I don't
mean more things, more fun, or more money.
Today, most have plenty of that to spare. I'm talking about
something deeper—something with eternal value.

Many young people are being shortchanged while we
compensate for broken homes, demanding careers, and selfish
pursuits. They are being given everything while starving for
a sense of worth, purpose, and connection. Our world gives
them mixed cues, which confuse their values, leaving them
without clear direction. Seeking, they turn to one thing or
another in an effort to fill the void that only God can fill.
We have left them spiritually barren.

Each generation seems to be a reaction to the last generation. Some turn away from traditional values to gain a sense of freedom. Others discard religion rather than accepting a genuine relationship with Christ. Some young people take a superior attitude toward Christian parents, viewing themselves as more enlightened and intelligent. What was once good is now seen as bad and vice versa. No wonder parents and grandparents are left shaking their heads in amazement at the turn of events.

As Christian parents and grandparents, what do our young people deserve from us? First of all, they deserve to be loved unconditionally. Don't push them away or reject them just because you may not agree with them. That doesn't mean we have to change our values or beliefs to appease them. We love them, *and* we hold on to God's truth.

Next, they deserve to be prayed for daily—earnestly and sincerely. This involves knowing them, caring about their lives, being happy for their successes, and being aware of their difficulties. It also means communicating this care to them by listening to them, taking time for them, and sharing our experiences with them.

As Christians, our young people deserve to see us living accountable lives. Many of us have made mistakes in the past, and those mistakes *do* impact our children. But it is never too late to do the right thing and to live in the right way. They need our example of righteous living. None of us is perfect, and we certainly don't want to be self-righteous, but genuine good living should be the goal for every one of us.

Our young people also deserve to know the gospel message. They need our testimony, both in word and deed, of what God has done for us. They deserve to know how much God loves them and the plan of salvation. They need us to gently lead them to Christ, knowing it is ultimately their choice to accept or reject Him as their Savior. No pressure, no beating them over the head—just love!

The Real Deal

Love must be sincere. Hate what is evil; cling to what is good.

—Romans 12:9 (NIV)

Have you known someone who you described as *the real deal?* You know, they just stood out in the crowd, not necessarily because they were talented or flashy but because they were *genuine*.

I attended the memorial service of a man I had never met. Yet, his life impacted me. As I listened to the stories of his family and friends, one after another, I came to the same conclusion. This man was the real deal. Although he was a humble man, he had led many to Christ over the years. In fact, the consensus was that he never passed up an opportunity to tell someone about the Savior, who he loved so dearly.

He was honored as a a father who prayed for his family as well as for many around the world. His concern for those on the fringe of society was notable. He had led many prisoners to Christ through his ministry, and his love for young people was displayed through his involvement in youth events. I watched as grown men spoke, with tears running down their cheeks, of the impact their friend, brother, father, or mentor had on their lives.

My husband had shared his own story with me earlier that day. During a ministry assignment, he and his friend were writing Bible study curriculum for teenagers. He looked up to see tears running down his friend's face. When he asked if he was all right, the answer was, "God's grace to us is so wonderful!"

I left the memorial service a little different than I had entered it—with my eyes more focused on Jesus, and my heart desiring to make more of a difference in my generation. Yes, this man who I had never met made an impact on my life that day, just as he had on the lives of countless others. That seems to be what happens when we have the good fortune and blessing of crossing paths with someone who is the real deal!

Being Transformed

And we all, who with unveiled faces contemplate the Lord's glory, are being transformed into his image with ever-increasing glory, which comes from the Lord, who is the Spirit.

—2 Corinthians 3:18 (NIV)

All of us need change when we become Christians. The scripture teaches that we are being transformed, little by little, throughout our lives. We cannot do this on our own. God has given us His Holy Spirit and His Word to help us become more like Christ. Although we can't accomplish this entirely in our own strength, we can cooperate with the process.

Inner purity, or sanctification, is the work of the Holy Spirit living inside of us. Although we desire to do what is right, we will still experience temptation. I am thankful God has given us His Spirit to enable us to resist temptations and to make right choices.

We will all fail at times, regardless of our best efforts. But our Heavenly Father, in His mercy and grace, has made provision for our failures. Ask for and receive God's forgiveness when you fail but don't be discouraged. Continue to purpose in your heart to be more like Christ and to learn from your mistakes.

None of us will reach perfection on this earth. So it's important to understand how God works in our lives to change and to transform us. At times, difficulties or tests may come, to help us grow up as believers. These difficulties strengthen us and are for our good. Rather than striving to make our life devoid of challenges, it is better to allow those challenges to build our fortitude and our faith as we are being transformed into the image of Christ!

Calming the Overactive Brain

Thou will keep *him* in perfect peace, *whose* mind *is* stayed
on thee: because he trusteth in thee.

—Isaiah 26:3 (KJV)

I attended a continuing education seminar on Calming the Overactive Brain, but it was mostly about depression and anxiety. The presenter was extremely knowledgeable in his field and did an excellent job presenting the material.

I learned some new things about the brain, but a lot of what was presented was *old hat* for me. I've treated problems from depression and anxiety for the past three decades, and most of the techniques that were presented to help these patients were ones I have already used. But I knew that God's Word also had something to say about the topic. Isaiah 26:3 kept going through my mind.

Of course, all of the scientific research is helpful, and treatments are beneficial, but there is more. The ageless wisdom of God's Word tells us how to handle our anxiousness.

The creator of the brain, with all of its intricate workings, promises to calm our anxieties as we focus on and put our trust in Him.

Scientists have actually studied this and have found that people who put their trust in God, during difficult times, have lower levels of the stress hormone cortisol than those who do not have faith. Our presenter shared numerous ways to reduce our stress reaction and calm our brains, such as healthy eating, exercise, and focusing on the present. He talked about different medications used to treat symptoms of anxiety and depression but also revealed their risks and limitations.

As a counselor, I have found various therapies to be helpful in alleviating symptoms and improving a person's stress response. Yet nothing comes close to the peace we have when trusting God and keeping our minds focused steadfastly on Him. Let's heed the wise counsel of our scientists and clinicians, but may we not underestimate the power of God's promise to calm us and keep us in *perfect peace*—something I have not heard any scientist or clinician claim to have achieved.

Laughter

A cheerful heart is good medicine, but a crushed spirit
dries up the bones.

—Proverbs 17:22 (NIV)

Do you laugh every day? Do you and your spouse laugh
together? I have to say, this was a priority for me when
I wrote out my "List of 44." This is the list of traits I asked
God for in a husband. Specifically, number seven on my list
says, "I would like him to have a sense of humor, to make me
laugh every day, and to see my humorous side."

I'm happy to say that my husband has made me laugh
almost every day since we've been married. Only a handful of
days have slipped by on a more somber note. Hey, nobody's
perfect! I realize that God is our true source of joy, but it's
definitely helpful to be able to laugh with your mate and to
share your inner joy with each other.

We all know that a happy heart does us good. And most
of us also know how devastating a broken heart can be.

God's Word encourages us to be joyful and to delight in all of our blessings.

I noticed an especially joyful woman one day. She seemed so happy and had a bubbly personality. I just assumed she must have had a wonderful life—until I later learned that she had had a less than perfect childhood and had gone through many difficult life experiences as an adult. I could hardly believe my ears. What an amazing work God had done in this sweet woman's heart. She wasn't bitter—she was thankful. She wasn't depressed—she was joyful.

My prayer is that we, as Christians, will live a life of joy. That doesn't necessarily mean we won't experience sadness or hurt, but it does mean we won't allow life's circumstances to rob us of our joy. It means we trust God enough to relax under the weight of life's pressures. Then we can enjoy the beautiful gift of laughter. It's good for the soul!

Are You an Agent of Encouragement or Discouragement?

> Therefore encourage one another and build each other up, just as in fact you are doing. Now we ask you, brothers and sisters, to acknowledge those who work hard among you, who care for you in the Lord and admonish you. Hold them in the highest regard in love because of their work. Live in peace with each other.
>
> —1 Thessalonians 5:11–13 (NIV)

Unfortunately, this passage in 1 Thessalonians does not always represent the state of affairs in our churches and ministries. Anyone can be an agent of criticism or discouragement. All it takes is having an opinion and believing it is your job to tell people just what you think about someone. Often this *someone* is a minister, a pastor, or a missionary.

Yet scripture admonishes us to hold those who are in the ministry in high regard and in love because of their work.

But you may ask, "What if I don't agree with them or don't like their style?" So what! They may not agree with you or like your style either, but that doesn't give any of us the license to become agents of discouragement. Romans 14:4 (NIV) says it well, "Who are you to judge the servant of another? To his own master he stands or falls; and he will stand, for the Lord is able to make him stand."

None of us has enough information to stand as another man's judge—only God does. So unless we want to play God, it is better to be agents of encouragement in the lives of others rather than cause disruption in the work of God. Our battles should be with the enemy of our soul, not with each other. Yet ministries often face their biggest battles from within. Our greatest fight should be to bring down the obstacles Satan puts in the way of winning souls to Christ— not to *bring down* or *put down* each other!

This has been something I have always disliked. I have heard people criticize certain ministers who God has used in one way or another to bless my life. My response has always been, "Well, I like _____." What else can I say? Each of us is entitled to our opinion, but I believe we often do the work of God a disservice by not keeping some of those hurtful and destructive opinions to ourselves. Why not pray for the person instead?

May God help all of us, as Christians, to become agents of encouragement rather than agents of discouragement in the lives of others. In so doing, the work of God will be advanced rather than hindered.

Why Not Complain?

And *when* the people complained, it displeased the Lord:
and the Lord heard *it*; and his anger was kindled.

—Numbers 11:1–2 (KJV)

We all do it, right? Some more than others! So why do we take so lightly something that scripture clearly says "kindled the anger of God?"

If we're not careful, negative thinking and complaining can become a habit. Repeated negative thoughts make it easier for other negative thoughts to come to us. Our brains then become wired to *seek* negativity.

We're all aware that chronic anger and frustration are not good for our health. The stress hormone, cortisol, can raise our blood pressure and increase our risk of heart disease and obesity. Studies indicate that optimistic people live longer than those with negative attitudes.

Recently, my husband and I walked out on a public dock to watch the sunset. Several people greeted us with hellos and smiles. My husband commented, "I like that … friendly people." Being such a positive and friendly person himself, he is naturally drawn to other positive people.

As we strolled by a photographer, who was capturing the sunset, my husband asked, "Did you get some good shots?"

I couldn't help but notice as the photographer proceeded to complain about the sunset. "Not colorful enough. I had hoped the sky would look better afterward."

I automatically responded, "It's still very pretty."

My husband and I have become connoisseurs of sunsets these days. We enjoy them, are often in awe of them, and sometimes just tell God that He is outdoing Himself. I have to admit that I was quite surprised to hear someone complain about a sunset. They're all different but beautiful.

I hope to never complain about a sunset or much else for that matter. I want to keep a positive attitude about life, daily giving thanks rather than grumbling and complaining. May God help each of us to be a bright, shining light of hope and gratitude as we live out our lives on this earth. May we continue to remind ourselves of all the reasons *not* to complain.

68

Fork in the Road

So Abram said to Lot, "Let's not have any quarreling between you and me, or between your herders and mine, for we are close relatives. Is not the whole land before you? Let's part company. If you go to the left, I'll go to the right; if you go to the right, I'll go to the left."

—Genesis 13:8–9 (NIV)

There are people who walk along beside us in our lives. They are a great blessing to us as we are to them. Then we come to a fork in the road, and they go one way and we go another—we take separate paths.

People come into our lives at different times for different reasons—to teach us, to help us, or to mature us. Each leaves his or her imprint on our soul, some more than others. This parting of ways can be sweet, bittersweet, or even heartbreaking. But the sooner we accept this as a natural part of life, the sooner we will be able to open our hearts to others, who will join us on our paths. Some will walk with us for a lifetime but others will not. Be assured that we will, again, come to a fork in the road. It is during these times that we learn to *let go* of what *was* and *embrace* what *is*.

It is here that we learn to look forward to what God has in store for us, even if it is not yet fully in our view. We learn to walk by faith, trusting God's goodness and wisdom. We learn to be thankful for those who have walked alongside us, for those who are walking with us today, and for those who will join us at our next fork in the road.

On Mission

The Lord was with Joseph so that he prospered, and he lived in the house of his Egyptian master. When his master saw that the Lord was with him, and that the Lord gave him success in everything he did, Joseph found favor in his eyes and became his attendant.

—Genesis 39:2–4 (NIV)

We are all on mission. When opposition comes, don't become discouraged. God allows things for our good. He is maneuvering us to the place of blessing and service he wants us to be in. So don't fret or worry when opposition comes. Don't fight it. Be patient, stay on mission, and be open to God's leading.

Joseph experienced opposition as God maneuvered him to a position of influence and great blessing. God used what was meant for evil to bring about ultimate good in his life. He used him to bless the very brothers who mistreated him. Joseph stayed on mission—serving God and praying for those who took evil action against him, and in the end, forgiving them and allowing God to use him to bless them. So let's not allow adverse circumstances to distract us from what God has called us to do. Let's stay on mission!

70

Beautiful Smiles

Religion that God our Father accepts as pure and faultless
is this: to look after orphans and widows in their distress
and to keep oneself from being polluted by the world.

—James 1:27 (NIV)

I knew I would have a soft spot in my heart for the children
living in the orphanages of Europe. As I looked around at
their smiling faces, some reminded me of kids we see in our
schools in the States.

I couldn't help but contrast the lifestyles of our youth to
these children. They are not living in luxury or abundance,
yet the smiles on their faces speak volumes. They were joyful
and so appreciative of what our ministry team brought to
them—games, fun, music, snacks, personal attention, and
the gospel message. We also brought our smiles and the love
of God flowing through us to them.

I recognized a few of the young people, who had been at
camp the previous summer. Many children and teens had

accepted Christ as their Savior during youth camp. The sporting events were a follow-up with them. You see, this ministry doesn't forget about them after the camp season is over. They go the extra mile—literally across the country—to show these children that they are important and valued.

During my visit, my husband and I stayed at the campgrounds in the village. I enjoyed the beautiful hillside views and the herds of sheep we met each day on our bumpy van ride into the village. During the week, I had the opportunity to learn more about the young ministry team. I found them to be fully dedicated to God and to sharing the gospel with the youth in their country.

It touched my heart to see many of the children and teens make decisions for Christ at the sporting events. Even though I didn't speak their language, I loved communicating with them in our own way—with our eyes, greetings, and smiles. I especially enjoyed one boy who wanted a little extra attention and spoke some English. He found a way to tease me and ask for extra snacks—with a smile, of course!

These children may not have all the possessions most kids take for granted, but that doesn't seem to keep them from enjoying life. They play, they have fun, and they *smile*!

Going the Extra Mile

Whoever forces you to go one mile, go with him two.

—Matthew 5:41 (NASB)

It's scriptural to go the extra mile, isn't it? It's very plainly written and requires no guesswork or deep interpretation. God's Word emphatically tells us that if we are required to go one mile, we should, instead, go *two*.

I saw this principle in action repeatedly during a mission trip to Europe. A young camp counselor joined us for a sports rally with children living in orphanages. When I asked the director if the teen's parents had driven him from his hometown, which had been a couple of hours away, his answer surprised me. "No, he hitchhiked all night to get here this morning."

I also found out that he had hitchhiked to our meetings earlier in the week. This had been about an eight-hour drive by car. The young man's dedication amazed me! He definitely went the extra mile to be part of this ministry.

I observed other examples of Christians going the extra mile. We literally drove across the country to let the orphan children know that they weren't forgotten. Many had accepted Christ at youth camp the previous summer. This ministry went the extra mile to have a sports rally for them, even though it involved many hours of travel on a winding two-lane road through mountainous areas. Not once did I hear a complaint.

I observed my husband also going the extra mile as he hobbled into a high school to speak to the eleventh and twelfth graders. He had injured his foot and was in a lot of pain, but you never would have known it as he spoke with a smile on his face. Six teens made life-changing decisions to accept Christ as their Savior when my husband gave the invitation.

There are many examples around us every day of people going the extra mile for others. May we, as Christians, look for opportunities to practice this principle in our daily lives—lovingly and without complaint.

Touching Experience

And pray in the Spirit on all occasions with all kinds of prayers and requests. With this in mind, be alert and always keep on praying for all the Lord's people.

—Ephesians 6:18 (NIV)

During a mission trip, my husband tore a ligament in his foot and was in a lot of pain before he received medical treatment. At first, he thought he had hurt it in some way and that it would just get better, so he continued with his speaking schedule as the pain increased each day.

During this time, the ministry team members had their evening meals at a local restaurant owned by a Christian family. They evidently noticed that my husband was limping more and more, each time we visited their establishment. One evening, the owner asked us to come back to the kitchen so the women could pray for him.

Two young women were cooking and cleaning but immediately stopped to come over to us. One woman knelt and touched my husband's ankle while she prayed. I couldn't help but notice her gentle face, almost like that of an angel.

Later that night, my husband said, "The woman who prayed for me had the face of an angel." We had both felt the Holy Spirit's presence during their prayers. My husband had tears in his eyes and told me that he had had a sensation in his ankle during the prayer. He said, "That was a special prayer."

These women took time from their busy schedule that evening to obey God's Word. They showed compassion for my husband and prayed for him. I will always have fond memories of that evening when God's people, in a restaurant kitchen in Europe, reached out in loving faith to pray for one of "the Lord's people."

PART 4

Praise

I will praise you, Lord my God, with all my heart; I will glorify your name forever.

—Psalm 86:12 (NIV)

My Prayer

Oh God, You desire our praise, The lifting of our voices, the raising of our hands, and the uplifting of our eyes and hearts to You, bring You glory. You delight in our genuine and humble thankfulness and in our recognition of Your blessings.

We ask for blessings but often fail to acknowledge them when they are given and take them for granted. Sometimes our eyes don't recognize the countless daily blessings and answers to prayer, which flow into our lives.

Why don't we see them? Why don't we acknowledge them? Why don't we give thanks for all of them?

As parents, we want our children to appreciate what we do for them, to say, "thank you," and to show us honor and respect. We don't want them to take us for granted or to merely feel entitled to more and more without appreciating what they have already received.

Heavenly Father, I believe You desire the same from us as Your children. You want us to seek relationship with You, not just to receive Your blessings. You want us to know You and honor and praise You for who You are and not just for what You can do for us. Yet, You also desire to give good gifts to your children.

Father, I ask that I will daily seek to have a deeper relationship with You. Even though I endeavor to seek You first, I ask that my eyes will be open to all the blessings You bring into my life and that my heart will be thankful for those blessings. I pray that my gratefulness will not only be expressed in praise to You but also in giving back to others. Amen.

May each of us remember to give praise to our heavenly Father for all of His blessings. May we not take them for granted but acknowledge them with gratitude. And may we also praise Him for who He *is*!

74

Knowing God Intimately

I will praise the Lord all my life; I will sing praise to my God as long as I live.

—Psalm 146:2 (NIV)

All of my life, as long as I live, I will praise God. The psalmist had a deep desire for God—to know Him, to love Him, and to praise Him. He wanted to know Him intimately!

Some of us miss the point, don't we? We become Christians and start going through the motions—attending church and trying to follow the rules. But there's more! And there's more than head knowledge. Our walk with God is a lifelong journey of getting to know Him, desiring Him, and loving Him more and more.

Once we taste of God's goodness, it both satisfies us and makes us hungry for more. You see, we don't become believers and stop there—with just a fond memory of our decision and the hope of heaven. Although this is so very important, it is not the totality of our Christian walk. It is the beginning. As a child is brought into the world, however glorious the experience, it is the *beginning*.

As believers, we begin our lifelong journey of knowing God by becoming intimate with Him. Let's not become complacent in the fact that we know God but instead, allow our knowing to be the catalyst for seeking to know Him even more. Let's remember to seek and praise Him *all* of our lives.

In Exodus 33:17–18 (NIV), the Lord said to Moses, "I will do the very thing you have asked, because I am pleased with you and I know you by name." Then Moses said, "Now show me your glory." May our desire for God be deep, and as Moses requested, may He show us His glory!

It's a New Day

The Lord's lovingkindnesses indeed never cease, for His compassions never fail. *They* are new every morning; Great is Your faithfulness.

—Lamentations 3:22–23 (NASB)

Have you ever had a sleepless night due to worry, stress, or an unresolved relationship issue? Most of us have. Then upon waking, we realize, *It's a new day—a fresh start!*

I've sometimes wondered if God gave us the division of night and day because He knew that, in all of our human imperfections and missteps, we would need to wake up to a new day—a day of new beginnings, second chances, forgiveness, and knowing that His lovingkindness, compassion, and faithfulness would never cease. They are new every morning! May God bless your journey today as you walk in the new day He has provided for you.

In the Morning

Let the morning bring me word of your unfailing love, for I have put my trust in you. Show me the way I should go, for to you I entrust my life.

—Psalm 143:8 (NIV)

I am in no way a morning person. I like to wake up leisurely and enjoy a few minutes of what I call "luxurious sleep." You know, those moments when we're half awake, still half asleep, and in a dreamlike state. Anyway, if you're actually a morning person, you probably have no idea what I'm talking about, but I do admire your morning energy!

I often tell my husband, who is a very early riser, that he conquers the day before I even get up in the morning. But I'm certainly not a lazy person. I get a lot done during my day. I just prefer to ease into it. Then I'm good to go!

Although I'm not a morning person, I still want to connect with my heavenly Father before I start my day. I want my thoughts to focus on His love. I want to put my trust in Him and ask for His guidance.

So in the morning, I have learned to say the words found in Psalm 143:8 (NIV), "Let the morning bring me word of your unfailing love, for I have put my trust in you. Show me the way I should go for to you I entrust my life." The psalmist's words remind me that I am entrusting my life to a loving God who is in control of every circumstance. I have found it to be true that a good way to start every single day is to read the Word of God—*in the morning!*

Bless the Lord

Bless the Lord, O my soul, And all that is within me, *bless* His holy name. Bless the Lord, O my soul, And forget none of His benefits.

—Psalm 103:1–2 (NASB)

In verse 3, the psalmist goes on to list the benefits he is referring to in Psalm 103:2. He tells us that the Lord pardons all of our iniquities and heals all of our diseases. Verse 4 assures us that He redeems our life from the pit and crowns us with lovingkindness and compassion. Verse 5 says that He satisfies our years with good things so that our youth is restored like the eagle's. What a list of benefits!

As you continue to read God's Word, you will find that the list goes on and on. Since we're told not to forget any of His benefits, I think it is helpful for us to discover just what those benefits are—not to make an idol of them but to be thankful and to "bless the Lord."

You see, we don't seek God for the purpose of receiving His benefits. We seek after Him because of who He is. Matthew 6:33 (NASB) tells us, "But seek ye first the kingdom of God, and His righteousness; and all these things shall be added unto you."

So let's bless the Lord with our praise and with a thankful heart. May we take time today to bless Him with all that is within us.

God Did Not Forget about You

For God so loved the world, that he gave his only begotten
Son, that whosoever believeth in him should not perish,
but have everlasting life.

—John 3:16 (KJV)

During one of our mission trips, I heard the most
beautiful testimony. It brought tears to my eyes as
a man told about being raised in an orphanage after his
parents had died. At age eighteen, he left the orphanage with
a big hole in his heart. The food and clothing didn't fill the
hole, that was left from unmet emotional needs. He told us
that most orphans leave this way—empty inside.

As a young adult, God reached out to him through a
friend's invitation to church. He accepted Christ and said
that afterward he heard the birds singing for the first time
and began to notice people smiling and laughing. He has
been walking with the Lord for over twenty years now.

I've heard many wonderful testimonies on the mission field. Everyone seems to come from a different place in life before they accept Christ. Some were raised in Christian homes and were led to Christ by their parents. Others came from different religious backgrounds and were ostracized by their families because of their decision to follow Jesus. Some have actually been kicked out of their own homes!

After hearing these testimonies, I realized I hadn't thought much about my own testimony, so I decided to sit down and write it out. This is my testimony.

I grew up in a home with parents who didn't attend church or profess to be Christians, but at an early age, a friend invited me to church with her family. I began attending regularly.

At age ten, I accepted Christ as my Savior, as a result of my friend's influence. I followed the Lord in baptism later that year. I'm still close to this childhood friend after having known each other for over fifty years. We're like sisters.

I believe God reached out His loving hands to me through my friend. She had been raised by Christian parents. Even though I didn't have the influence of a Christian home, God did not forget about me. I'm so thankful He didn't forget about me.

I attended church every time the doors were open and started a small Bible study at school during my fifth-grade year. I read my Bible every day and felt Jesus walking close to me. Family and school friends sometimes teased me for praying before meals and going to church so much. But I didn't care. I felt the Holy Spirit strengthening me as I followed Christ.

As a teenager, I attended Christian youth camps for several summers and loved it! When I was fifteen years old, my twelve-year-old brother became ill with leukemia. I had the privilege of sharing the gospel with him and leading him to Christ before he died. God did not forget about him.

Many of you may have grown up in a home where you didn't have the opportunity to be led to Christ by your parents. He still loves you so much that He died for you and reached out His loving arms to you. You have the opportunity to accept Him as your Savior. He has not forgotten about you!

The Privilege of His Presence

Don't you know that you yourselves are God's temple and that God's Spirit dwells in your midst.

—1 Corinthians 3:16 (NIV)

Adam and Eve had daily, close fellowship with God until they sinned. He came down and walked and talked with them in the garden. They became afraid and hid from the presence of God because of their sin. Then they were banished.

Can you imagine the loss they must have felt? They had lost their privilege of God's presence. We also remain in a state of separation from God until we, through faith, accept Christ as our Savior. Our sins are forgiven, and we are no longer separated from His presence.

Yet we often take this privilege for granted. We have the luxury of waking up each morning and saying, "Good morning!" to our Creator. We can converse with Him about our day as we drive to work. We can acknowledge

His beautiful handiwork in nature by complimenting His exquisite creativity.

Just think about it for a minute. It's a great privilege, isn't it? But we've become a bit spoiled by the lavishness of God's blessings on us. We simply take things for granted.

My first mission trip made me aware of some of the simple *privileges* I took for granted: ice tea, a clothes dryer, and air conditioning, to name a few. When I got back home I looked at those things with a newfound appreciation.

Sometimes those who have been saved from the most sinful of lives seem to greatly appreciate God's grace. But those of us who have been in church for years have to guard against taking things for granted. We have to remind ourselves just how privileged we are—not by our own merits but by the grace of God.

So when we wake up tomorrow morning, let's remember the wonderful privilege we have of walking in the presence of our heavenly Father. Let us greet Him, talk with Him throughout the day, thank Him, and bask in His love. Let's not forget the *privilege of His presence.*

The Power of the Gospel

For I am not ashamed of the gospel of Christ: for it is the
power of God unto salvation to everyone that believeth;

—Romans 1:16 (KJV)

When something *jumps out at me*, I jot it down so I can
go back and reflect on it later. The message I heard
raised the question as to why some believers don't share the
gospel with others. Is it because they're not confident in the
power of the gospel? I hadn't thought of it that way, but it
makes sense. Why would we hold back something so life
changing if we had full confidence in its power?

Yet as Christians, we might deny this and say, "Of course,
we believe in the power of the gospel." But what do our
actions say? Let's at least give it some thought. We don't have
to be confident in our own speaking ability to share God's
plan of salvation. It's not about us having favor with people or
having charisma. It's about not being ashamed of the gospel
of Christ and knowing it is the power of God unto salvation.

What a privilege we have to be the bearer of this good news to others. So let's renew our confidence and start impacting our world for Christ! May God bless each of us as we, in full confidence, take His message of salvation to a lost world.

Exquisite

However, if you suffer as a Christian, do not be ashamed,
but praise God that you bear that name.

—1 Peter 4:16 (NIV)

"It's quite an exquisite thing to be a Christian—to carry
His name." I had never heard it stated like this before,
but the words resonated with me!

Exquisite is a descriptive word, which means extremely
beautiful, lovely, or fine. Yes, that certainly describes
Christ and His relationship with us! His love and sacrifice
for us is exquisite. His presence with us, His promises to
us, and our walk with Him are nothing short of extremely
beautiful.

I say this knowing full well that in this world we will have
trouble, but He has overcome the world! I can say this even
though we will all face death because He has overcome the
grave! How about living our lives with the hope of eternal
life before us? How exquisite is that?

I praise God for the privilege of bearing the name of Christ. I am not ashamed to be a Christian and am in full agreement with the words I heard that day. "It is quite an exquisite thing to be a Christian."

82

Let's Pray

In the same way the Spirit also helps our weakness; for we do not know how to pray as we should, but the Spirit Himself intercedes for *us* with groanings too deep for words; and He who searches the hearts knows what the mind of the Spirit is, because He intercedes for the saints according to *the will of* God.

—Romans 8:26–27 (NASB)

I recently spent the weekend at a mission conference, and my heart was touched. I came away feeling refreshed and inspired.

Along with the congregation's hospitality and enthusiasm for missions, the guest speaker's message deeply touched my heart. A mature, soft-spoken missionary presented Romans 8:26–27 in a way that I had never heard emphasized, and yet, his words rang with power and truth.

I have understood the scripture that tells us the Holy Spirit intercedes for the saints according to the will of God, but what I had missed is that this happens *every* time we pray. The Holy Spirit helps our weakness because we don't know how to pray as we should. We don't know how to pray according to the will of God, but the Holy Spirit does.

This intercession takes place *when* we pray and not when we don't. What I'm saying is that this message has made me want to pray more—knowing that God takes my weakness (not knowing how to pray) and infuses it with the power of the Holy Spirit, who intercedes for us according to the will of God. This produces results.

The speaker told us that the Holy Spirit sifts through our prayers, sifts through the unnecessary parts (you know, the flowery words, etc.), and presents them to God for us. Although there are times when I certainly *feel* the Holy Spirit moving on my heart, I now realize that He is helping me every time I pray and doing His work of interceding for the saints. So with that powerful truth in mind—let's pray!

God Has Prepared Good Things for Us

For we are his workmanship, created in Christ Jesus for good works, which God prepared beforehand so that we would walk in them.

—Ephesians 2:10 (NASB)

A group of us were having lunch after a morning of ministering in a high school where six decisions for Christ were made. During our meal, one young man talked about how God had prepared good things for us. We talked about our lives and the privilege of serving God in a ministry to the youth of Europe. Afterward, this young man's words stayed with me as I pondered their meaning.

So what did this mean to me? As I searched scripture, I found that I had been created in Christ Jesus for good works, which God had prepared beforehand for me. But I had to make the choice to walk in them.

Looking back on my life, I see times when I walked in those good works and times when I thought my own ways were best. At this time in my life, after pressing into God, seeking His will above my own, and listening carefully for His voice, I clearly see the contrast. The things He prepared for me were so much better than those I had planned for myself. My prayer is that each of us will understand what a great privilege it is to walk in the good works our heavenly Father has prepared for us.

High and Lifted Up

And I, if I be lifted up from the earth, will draw all *men* unto me.

—John 12:32 (KJV)

Scripture tells us that Jesus said these words to signify how He would die. He was lifted up on the cross and suffered a painful death as the sacrificial lamb for the sins of the world. He told us that, if He was lifted up, He would draw all men unto Himself.

Because of His sacrifice, all people are invited to receive forgiveness of their sins, right relationship with God, and eternal life in heaven. We celebrate Good Friday as a remembrance of Christ's death on the cross. We lift Him up.

As Christians, we have the privilege of lifting Jesus up every day of the year and not just during the Easter season. We do this by worshiping Him, sharing our testimonies, and living in a way that honors Him. As we seek to follow Christ's teachings and walk in love, He is glorified. We lift

Him up when we take the gospel to those who have not heard it.

We aren't the ones who draw men to Christ, but when they finally see Him, they are drawn to Him by the Holy Spirit. May our lives illuminate the darkness, giving enough light for others to clearly see Him—high and lifted up.

He Came Down from Heaven

For I have come down from Heaven, not to do My own
will, but the will of Him who sent Me.

—John 6:38 (NASB)

Can you visualize the day when Christ took off His
royal robe and laid aside His crown so He could come
down here and get us—rescue us—and save us? When I
heard these words, tears came to my eyes as I visualized the
scenario in my mind. This is an amazing truth, and yet, I
had never thought of it quite this way.

He humbled Himself, left His heavenly home to come
and walk on the earth, and died an excruciating death on the
cross for you and for me. Words cannot describe this kind
of love. Yet many still reject His sacrifice and His love. Jesus
humbled Himself to do His Father's will. Yet many refuse
to humble themselves to raise a hand or walk an aisle when
they hear the invitation to accept Him as their Savior. My
prayer is that you will not allow your pride to keep you from
running into His outstretched arms.

He Is Risen

There was a violent earthquake, for an angel of the Lord came down from heaven and, going to the tomb, rolled back the stone and sat on it. His appearance was like lightning, and his clothes were white as snow. The guards were so afraid of him that they shook and became like dead men. The angel said to the women, "Do not be afraid, for I know that you are looking for Jesus, who was crucified. He is not here; he has risen, just as he said. Come and see the place where he lay."

—Matthew 28:2–6 (NIV)

He is risen! Have you taken the time to think about all that Christ's resurrection means to you? I've thought about it, but I'm sure in my limited human perspective, I am missing some of it. I don't believe we will fully comprehend all that the resurrection entails until we leave this earth for our heavenly home. We won't completely understand the magnitude of His power and love until we see Him in all of His glory.

What I do know is that because He has risen, I have the promise of eternal life. That's something to celebrate! Yet sometimes we get more excited about a football game than we do about our eternal hope. Again, our human minds don't fully understand.

I have a suspicion that once we arrive in heaven, we will look back on our earthly life and shake our heads at how insignificant most of the things we got excited about actually were. I think we will realize how off focus our sight was on things of eternal value. We might think, *If I knew then what I know now, I would have lived my life as a celebration of all that His resurrection means.* I hope each Easter season will remind us of Christ's loving sacrifice, the power of His resurrection, and our eternal hope. May we see Him as He is—our *risen* Savior!

Rejection

Because I called and you refused, I stretched out my hand and no one paid attention; And you neglected all my counsel and did not want my reproof;

—Proverbs 1:24–25 (NASB)

*N*one of us like rejection! In fact, most of us go to great lengths to avoid it, don't we? Our spirits are crushed when we are rejected by someone we love—a close friend, a family member, or our sweetheart. Yet over and over, scripture refers to God being rejected by those He loves—by His own creation.

God reached out to us by sending His Son to be our Savior. Again, more rejection! The Bible tells us that His chosen people, the Israelites, rejected His counsel and ignored His reproof. Over and over again, they strayed from God to follow their own ways and to do what they wanted.

It almost sounds like what some parents go through with their children, doesn't it? Yet our heavenly Father won't give up on us. He keeps reaching out His hand to us, all the while knowing He will continue to be rejected by many. He loves us that much. Christ came into this world knowing He would be rejected and even despised by people. Yet there is rejoicing in heaven over each one who accepts Him.

The story of the prodigal son says it well. A rejected father runs with open arms when his son returns home after leaving his father's house to squander his inheritance. The father lovingly receives him and rejoices over him, putting aside his own hurt and rejection. Our heavenly Father does the same for each of His children who return to Him.

I hope we realize what a wonderful, loving, heavenly Father we have. I pray we will seek Him, value His counsel, hear His voice when He calls, and respond to His outstretched hand.

Shepherd of My Soul

I am the good shepherd; the good shepherd lays down His life for the sheep.

—John 10:11 (NASB)

As we drove through the countryside of Romania one spring day, I caught a glimpse of a herd of sheep on the hillside. This sight, in itself, would not have been all that unusual for me (We have sheep in the States), but it was the shepherd who stood out to me. Dressed in a long garment and with staff in hand, he stood peacefully watching over his sheep.

My thoughts went immediately to Jesus, my Shepherd—the Shepherd of my soul. A sense of peace filled me as I thought of Him gently watching over us. The shepherd on the hill wasn't frantically running about, trying to get his sheep to move here or there or to do this or that. He was gently guiding them with his staff. The sheep weren't nervously moving about in fear or unrest. They were quiet and still, seemingly calmed by the very presence of their shepherd.

Jesus is our "good shepherd." He laid down His life for us. He tells us not to be afraid but to trust in Him, to follow Him, and to rest in Him.

I'm thankful for the visual I saw that day in Romania of the shepherd with his sheep. It helped me turn my thoughts from the busyness of my everyday life to the beautiful gift I have in Jesus—the Shepherd of my soul.

Faith

Now faith is the substance of things hoped for, the evidence of things not seen.

—Hebrews 11:1 (KJV)

Substance. Evidence. Those are concrete words, yet we often think of faith as abstract or something we believe.

Substance is the real physical matter of which a person or thing consists, and which has a tangible presence. *Evidence* is the available body of facts indicating whether a belief is true. And *Faith* is complete trust or confidence in someone or something.

Based on these definitions, how strong is your faith when you pray? I've had to ask myself this question many times. Sometimes we spend so much time second-guessing whether or not what we're praying about is God's will, we end up watering down our faith to the point of ineffectiveness.

James 5:16 (KJV) tells us, "Confess *your* faults one to another, and pray one for another, that ye may be healed.

The effectual fervent prayer of a righteous man availeth much." That doesn't sound like weak faith to me.

I personally think we have to pray specifically rather than generally regarding our needs. *Substance* and *evidence* are very specific words, and since faith means complete trust and confidence, we have to know specifically who or what we are having complete confidence in.

God is sovereign and doesn't always answer our prayers the way we want. But that doesn't mean we can't have strong faith. It means we ought to pray, believing for answers to our prayers but at the same time, having complete trust and confidence in the sovereignty of God.

This past year, I have seen some amazing answers to many specific prayers. Some have involved ongoing changes in people and circumstances while others could be viewed as miracles. Some requests have been answered with a "no" or a "not yet"—all in the sovereignty of God. Regardless of the visible outcomes, I will continue to pray because I have full confidence and trust in the *One* I am praying to.

Miracles Are Everywhere

You are the God who performs miracles; you display your power among the peoples.

—Psalm 77:14 (NIV)

I was deeply touched by the movie *Miracles from Heaven*, which I saw recently. As I was driving to the theatre, I was thinking, *Miracles are all around us. Actually, they're everywhere!*

The couple in the movie had experienced the beautiful miracle of their young daughter being healed by God of a medically incurable disease. But in the end, the girl's mother came to the conclusion that miracles are everywhere. If we aren't living our lives in awe of the daily miracles all around us, we are truly missing out. We are missing out on living a joyful, thankful, and blessed life.

Tears came to my eyes several times during this movie as I watched a mother struggle with her faith because of the pain her child was suffering. She couldn't understand God's purposes in allowing her family to go through this storm. Yet in the end, so many lives were touched, and people saw God's hand at work. Miracles took place all around the family before the child ever received her physical healing.

A miracle is defined as something that cannot be explained by the natural laws of our world, but I see even those laws of nature as a miracle. Look around you. What do you see? I saw a magnificent sunset spread across the sky as I was driving home that evening. Was that not a miracle? Does the fact that it happens every day make it any less of a miracle? I think not. How about the people we see every day? Aren't we all really a miracle when you think about it?

It's easy to be in awe of a miracle that transcends our human reasoning, yet we pass right by many miracles every day without giving them a second thought or glance. We miss out as we get caught up in our busy lives, our worries, and our apathy. I pray that God will help us to slow down and open our eyes to see His miracles. They're *everywhere*.

Sharing Our Faith

> Then he said to his disciples, "The harvest is plentiful but the workers are few. Ask the Lord of the harvest, therefore, to send out workers into his harvest field."
>
> —Matthew 9:37–38 (NIV)

Why are we so hesitant to share our faith with others? While seemingly at ease discussing such matters with fellow believers, we tend to leave our testimonies out of other conversations. Why? Do we fear we will impose ourselves on others and will upset them, or is it our own pride—wanting to fit in and be accepted?

The Bible says the harvest is great, but do we see it, or do we choose to put blinders on as we go about our daily lives? This gives us a false sense of comfort, doesn't it? The blinders allow us to see our neighbor's smiling face as he waves to us each day. They allow us to think, "He's doing well. He's okay." Our blinders allow us not to feel compassion for his soul. They keep us from praying for him or sharing our faith with him. We wave back and go on our way with no concern about where our friendly neighbor will spend eternity.

People need us to care *first* and then share our faith with them. Our words won't touch their hearts unless they know we genuinely care about them. We automatically assume people will be closed and won't accept Christ as their Savior. But these assumptions are faulty. People are hurting in our world today. They are searching for something to fill the void in their lives that only Christ can fill.

So share your faith. Do a personal inventory to identify what attitudes and assumptions are holding you back, then prayerfully seek God's direction. Ask Him to open your eyes to the great harvest and dedicate yourself to be a laborer in that harvest. God wants to use your life and personal testimony to impact the lives of others for *eternity.*

Be Prepared

But in your hearts revere Christ as Lord. Always be prepared to give an answer to everyone who asks you to give the reason for the hope that you have. But do this with gentleness and respect.

1 Peter 3:15 (NIV)

Lately, I've thought a lot about what it means to share my faith with others. I've heard several sermons about the subject and have written down my own thoughts. My question seems to be, "How can I be prepared to give the reason for the hope I have in Christ?"

I heard a sermon on this topic and learned about the iPhone app called *Life on Mission*. I downloaded it and studied the conversation guide. It starts with God's original design and how man's sin led to brokenness. When we repent and believe as a result of hearing the gospel, we recover from our brokenness and pursue God's original design of a right relationship with Him.

I also attended a workshop called, The God Test. This was another iPhone app with more involved training. It is also a conversation tool to engage others in a discussion about God and about the gospel. The app offers detailed training to assist in reaching others with the good news of salvation.

The seminar presenter stressed the importance of showing care and respect toward those we are talking to. He told us not to be weird about it. If someone says, "I'm not interested," just shake that person's hand, thank him or her, and tell that individual to have a nice day.

Don't assume people won't be open to a discussion of their beliefs about God. Many simply don't know what they believe in.

So as you can see, I'm trying to be better prepared to give an answer to others as to why I trust in Jesus as my Lord and Savior—to give the reason for my hope. I pray God will help us, as Christians, prepare ourselves to gently and respectfully lead others to Christ. May those around us not only hear the good news but also believe and receive God's precious gift of salvation.

93

Leading Others to Christ

The fruit of the righteous *is* a tree of life; and he that winneth souls *is* wise.

—Proverbs 11:30 (KJV)

Sometimes we think this is what ministers do but not us. Can you visualize yourself holding someone's hand and walking toward Jesus—literally leading them to Christ?

I have had the opportunity to directly lead a handful of people to Christ during my lifetime, but looking back, I think it could have been more. What holds us back? Maybe in our younger years, it's shyness or not wanting to offend someone. But the Bible clearly gives each of us, as Christians, the great commission to share the gospel.

I had the opportunity to see many young people accept Christ after my husband had spoken in camp meetings in Europe. I also watched him witness to others one-on-one. As a missionary, he has been instrumental in reaching hundreds and even thousands of people for Christ over the years.

On the anniversary of his own decision to follow Christ, he wrote a beautiful message describing his experience. My heart was touched by his sincere words: "Trusted Christ and accepted Him into my heart and life fifty years ago. God has been incredibly good to me through various experiences in life—more than I deserve! If you are one of my friends who has never made this decision, I warmly encourage you to do so right now."

Here is a prayer you can use in case you don't know what to do or say:

Dear God, I realize that I am a sinner, and I ask you to forgive me of my sins. I now believe that Jesus Christ is Your Son and trust that He gave His life for me. I believe that you raised Him from the grave. Come into my heart and life. I turn away from my former life and give my heart and life completely to you. Thank you for accepting me and saving me from my sins. Amen.

My husband is truly a soul winner at heart. He has allowed God to work through him to reach others for Christ. He is a willing vessel. You may say, "But he's a minister." We may not reach the crowds, but we all can reach one, or five, or ten.

While on another mission trip, I attended the local Spanish-speaking church for its Sunday morning service. One of the women interpreted most of the message for me. Something the music leader said stood out to me. He told us we were privileged to be able to share the gospel with others. Even the angels couldn't do this. It was *our* privilege! I had never considered the idea that the angels couldn't share the gospel with people during this dispensation. It truly is our privilege to do so.

I pray that each of us will seek to win souls for Christ. I know many of us plant the seeds, and another reaps the harvest. But let's all endeavor to reach our world for Christ.

94

The Angels Rejoice

In the same way, I tell you, there is joy in the presence of the angels of God over one sinner who repents.

—Luke 15:10 (NASB)

My heart has been so touched each time young people have come to Christ at the mission youth camps. Since joining my husband in his life's work as a missionary to youth in Europe and Costa Rica, I have had many rich experiences. It has been a joy to work alongside other Christians who minister to young people.

Jesus tells us there is rejoicing in heaven over every single one of us when we repent and accept Christ as our Savior. Can you visualize the celebration? It's most likely beyond our comprehension! This tells us how important we are to God, how much He loves us, and how precious our salvation is to Him.

During one camp service, I sat with tears welling up in my eyes as seventy-four of the seventy-five campers went forward to accept Christ. In Romania, they are called "repenters" in a derogatory manner by unbelievers. Yet the angels rejoice over each one who repents.

I know my heart will continue to be touched each time I see a young person go forward to accept Christ. I want to be sure to remember the celebration simultaneously going on in heaven. May we all rejoice together!

How Great Is His Love?

Greater love has no one than this: to lay down one's own life for one's friends.

—John 15:13 (NIV)

Just how great is God's love for us? He laid down His life to give us eternal life—amazing!

On special occasions like holidays, birthdays, and anniversaries, we think about the ones we love. We buy cards or gifts to express how we feel about our spouses, family members, and friends. All of this is fun and makes us feel warm toward each other, and that's great. But I would like us to go a step further and think about Christ's love for us. It's hard to fully comprehend this type of sacrificial love, isn't it?

During the first night of a youth camp, a teenager came up to my husband after the service. He thanked him for his message and said it had really helped him. My heart was touched by his sincerity.

The next night, that teen went forward to accept Christ as his Savior during the invitation. At the campfire meeting later in the week, he was one of the first to fully dedicate his life to God. Tears came to my eyes as I watched every single camper stand around the campfire weeping before the Lord. I remembered when I had done the same at a Christian youth camp many years ago.

On the final morning of camp, the young teen went forward again, this time to give his testimony of what God had done for him that week. I learned that he did not attend church and had been invited to camp by another young man. He hadn't known any of the other kids before that, but had made new friends.

In my own testimony, I have written how thankful I am that God didn't forget about me. Not only did Jesus die for me but God also provided a way for me to hear the gospel, even though my family didn't go to church. I couldn't help but think of how much Jesus loved this young man who had not been raised in a Christian home. God did not forget about him. *How great is His love for us!*

96

By Grace

For by grace you have been saved through faith; and that not of yourselves, *it is* the gift of God; not as a result of works, so that no one may boast.

—Ephesians 2:8–9 (NASB)

A young teen came forward to accept Christ at the end of a youth camp service, but when she later spoke with her camp counselor, she felt she couldn't be saved because her "works" weren't good enough. She felt she had to have faith but also have acceptable behavior before she could receive salvation.

I sometimes hear parents tell their children to be really good so they can go to heaven. But God meets us right where we are when we accept Christ as our Savior. In other words, we simply cannot earn salvation. There would have been no need for Christ's sacrifice if we could have been perfect.

When we come to Christ and ask forgiveness for our sins, we are repenting. Genuine repentance involves being willing to turn from our sin and to follow Him. We can't do this in our own strength, but the Bible tells us we produce spiritual fruit by abiding in the vine. Christ is the vine.

He empowers us to live for Him. That doesn't mean we will be perfect. We won't. It does mean we need to focus on having a close relationship with Him and to allow the Holy Spirit to work in our lives. If we sin, we have an advocate with the father—Jesus Christ!

This doesn't mean we accept Christ as our Savior and then go on living a sinful life. We serve Him out of love. God wants to have a loving relationship with us and for us to love each other. He gives us the gift of salvation to either accept or reject. By grace we are saved, through faith.

Lift Up Your Hands

Lift up your hands in the sanctuary and praise the Lord.

—Psalm 134:2 (NIV)

May my prayer be set before you like incense; may the lifting up of my hands be like the evening sacrifice.

—Psalm 141:2 (NIV)

I will praise you as long as I live, and in your name I will lift up my hands.

—Psalm 63:4 (NIV)

Have you ever been in a worship service where you sincerely felt like lifting your hands in praise to God but didn't? You held back. Maybe you didn't want to draw attention to yourself, or perhaps it felt awkward because this wasn't a common practice in your particular church. Yet God's Word clearly tells us to lift up our hands, not only when we are worshipping alone at home but "in the sanctuary."

I'm addressing this issue because I am one of those who sometimes "holds back" and doesn't lift my hands in praise to God—even when my spirit is humbly moved to do so. Although I grew up in an atmosphere where raising our hands in worship was completely accepted as an appropriate expression of worship, some of the settings I have been in over the years have been more reserved. I'm not criticizing those settings, but I am taking a look at what it means for me to worship authentically.

I've decided that some of it is my own personality. I'm a bit reserved until I get to know you. Then I might be on the floor playing trains with my grandson or chasing him through the house. You get the picture—unreservedly enjoying myself! Maybe it's a pride thing. If that's the case, I need to get over myself.

There is always a counterfeit for everything. That being said, let's not allow the fear of being perceived as a fake to keep us from humbly worshipping our Lord with hands raised, at times, when it comes from our heart.

Each of us has our own personal relationship with our heavenly Father. Many worship from their heart and never consider raising their hands toward heaven. That is certainly a personal choice, and we know that God receives our praise. He looks at our hearts.

But for those of us who desire to lift our hands to God in worship but have held back for various reasons, maybe it is time to prayerfully search our hearts. Why not set aside the barriers we have erected and humbly and authentically draw near to God in worship. Let's make it about Him and not about us as we *lift up our hands in the sanctuary and praise the Lord.*

The Holy Spirit

And I will pray the Father, and he shall give you another Comforter, that he may abide with you forever; Even the Spirit of truth; whom the world cannot receive, because it seeth him not, neither knoweth him: but ye know him; for he dwelleth with you, and shall be in you.

—John 14: 16-17 (KJV)

As Christians, we know that God has sent His Holy Spirit to dwell in us. We are told that the Spirit intercedes for us when we pray. He intercedes for us according to the will of God. What a beautiful gift God has given us. Our heavenly Father knows we don't always know how to pray, so He has given us a helper.

I think it is important to understand the work of the Holy Spirit in our lives and to see this as a natural part of walking in the Spirit. As scripture teaches us, it is not by our own might or power but by His Spirit that we live victorious Christian lives. My husband often says that the older he gets, the more he realizes that, without God, he can do absolutely nothing. God has gifted him as a speaker, singer, and evangelist, but he acknowledges God as his source of strength.

Sometimes we try to live the Christian life in our own strength and flesh. It doesn't work! We get weary, weak, burned out, or even prideful. God's Word teaches us, over and over, to walk in the Spirit, pray in the Spirit, and rely on the Holy Spirit to teach, guide, and comfort us. We can't live a spiritual life in the flesh any more than we can live a worldly life in the Spirit. Water and oil don't mix. So let's be thankful, not only for God's gift of salvation through Christ but also for His gift of the Holy Spirit.

Hope of Heaven

But as it is written, Eye hath not seen, nor ear heard, neither have entered into the heart of man, the things which God hath prepared for them that love him.

—1 Corinthians 2:9 (KJV)

As I'm coming toward the end of this devotional book, I want to draw attention to our hope of heaven. We have this hope because of the sacrificial death and resurrection of Jesus. The Bible tells us in 1 John 1:9 (KJV), "If we confess our sins, he is faithful and just to forgive us *our* sins, and to cleanse us from all unrighteousness." Jesus told His disciples that He was going to prepare a place for them so they could be where He was.

I've tried to imagine what heaven is like, haven't you? When we lose a loved one to death, our interest is piqued. When my son and daughter grew up and went away to college or when they moved to a new place, it wasn't long until I had to go for a visit. I wanted to see where they lived so that whenever I thought of them, I could picture them in their surroundings. When a loved one *moves to heaven*, it is natural for us to want to be able to visualize them in their new home.

Scripture tells us that no matter how hard we try to imagine what awaits us in heaven, what God has prepared for us hasn't even entered our hearts yet. Try as we might, we cannot fully comprehend the splendor of heaven because *nothing* on earth can compare to it. Yet as Christians, we have this beautiful hope of heaven to look forward to. It is the hope of eternal life in God's presence. There will be no more tears, no more pain, *and* no more death!

Worship

But thou *art* holy, *O thou* that inhabitest the praises of Israel.

—Psalm 22:3 (KJV)

I wanted to finish my devotional writings in this book with an emphasis on worship. The Bible tells us that God inhabits the praise of His people and that He is worthy to receive our worship. In the book of Revelation, heaven is described as a place that is exploding with continual worship, music, and voices raised in praise to a Holy God.

Here on earth, we see God's hand at work the most in the midst of our praise as prayers are answered, the sick are healed, and hearts are changed. God manifests His power as He inhabits our praise. He is at home there!

Have you ever been in a worship service where you literally felt God's presence all around you so strongly you wanted to reach out and touch Him? Sometimes I get goose bumps when this happens. Other times, it's simply a sweet sense of His gentle presence.

Let's not forget the importance of taking time to humble ourselves before our God in worship. There are so many things to do in this life and so much to keep us busy and distracted. Yet not only does God desire our praise, He also desires an intimate relationship with us. *And* we are changed—in His presence!

Conclusion

I hope you have been blessed by reading my devotional writings and have gleaned some wisdom from them for your own life as well. They are meant to be an encouragement to you, as we share so many common experiences in this life. I am deeply grateful for the gifts God has given me—gifts of faith, hope, courage, and new beginnings. My prayer is that your faith will be strengthened, your hope renewed, and your courage bolstered as you look forward to all the new beginnings God has for you!

About the Author

Stephanie Murphy offers encouragement to us as we maneuver the twists and turns of life, grieve our losses, and find our own new beginnings. She draws not only on her three decades of experience as a family therapist but also on her personal experiences. Stephanie also shares wisdom from God's Word and from her own Christian faith.

She has a master's degree in counseling and is a licensed marriage and family therapist. Stephanie is actively involved with her husband in his life's work as a missionary to young people in Europe. Having survived the death of a spouse, she has learned to press into God during difficult circumstances and understands what it means to find renewed faith, hope, and courage for all of life's new beginnings.

Stephanie is also the author of *Strong and Courageous: Encouragement for Families Touched by Autism*, WestBow Press, 2017.

Printed in the United States
By Bookmasters